Religion and the Arts in *The Hunger Games*

Brill Research Perspectives in Religion and the Arts

Editor-in-Chief

Aaron Rosen (*Wesley Theological Seminary, Washington, DC*)

Associate Editors

Barbara Baert (*University of Leuven*)
Yohana A. Junker (*Pacific School of Religion, Berkeley*)
S. Brent Plate (*Hamilton College, New York*)
Zhange Ni (*Virginia Tech*)

Founding Editor

Diane Apostolos-Cappadona (*Georgetown University, Washington, DC*)

Volumes published in this Brill Research Perspectives title are listed at *brill.com/rpra*

Religion and the Arts in *The Hunger Games*

By

Zhange Ni

BRILL

LEIDEN | BOSTON

This paperback book edition is simultaneously published as issue 4.1 (2020) of *Brill Research Perspectives in Religion and the Arts*, DOI: 10.1163/24688878-12340011.

Library Congress Control Number: 2020921328

Typeface for the Latin, Greek, and Cyrillic scripts: "Brill". See and download: brill.com/brill-typeface.

ISBN 978-90-04-44893-3 (paperback)
ISBN 978-90-04-44913-8 (e-book)

Copyright 2020 by Zhange Ni. Published by Koninklijke Brill NV, Leiden, The Netherlands.
Koninklijke Brill NV incorporates the imprints Brill, Brill Hes & De Graaf, Brill Nijhoff, Brill Rodopi, Brill Sense, Hotei Publishing, mentis Verlag, Verlag Ferdinand Schöningh and Wilhelm Fink Verlag.
Koninklijke Brill NV reserves the right to protect this publication against unauthorized use. Requests for re-use and/or translations must be addressed to Koninklijke Brill NV via brill.com or copyright.com.

This book is printed on acid-free paper and produced in a sustainable manner.

Contents

Religion and the Arts in *The Hunger Games* 1
    Zhange Ni
    Abstract 1
    Keywords 1
  1 Introduction 1
  2 Enchantment I: Sovereign Power and Ritual Sacrifice 8
    2.1 *Inventing Panem: Sovereign Power and Bare Life* 9
    2.2 *Creating the Sacred through Ritual Sacrifice* 16
    2.3 *Another Sacrifice Is Possible* 20
  3 Enchantment II: Bare Life and the Religion/Art of Resistance 23
    3.1 *Katniss the Singer and the Spirituality of Music* 24
    3.2 *The Mimetic Art of Peeta the Painter* 31
    3.3 *Mockingjay, the Image at Work* 35
  4 The Split Enchantment of *The Hunger Games* Reality Show 38
    4.1 *Reality TV: The Entertaining Real* 38
    4.2 The Hunger Games *Show: Nazi Camp and Disneyland* 43
    4.3 *The Unclosed Real and the Tactics of the Powerless* 46
    4.4 *Rethinking Religion and Media in the Age of Reality TV* 49
  5 The Split Enchantment of Food and Clothing, the Game of Hungers 52
    5.1 *Food and Clothing: Foodways and Fashion Systems* 53
    5.2 *Food and Clothing: The Game of Hungers beyond the Arenas* 56
    5.3 *Food, Clothing, and the Material Turn in the Study of Religion* 63
  6 The Split Enchantment of *The Hunger Games* Transmedia Assemblage 67
    6.1 *Transmedia Storytelling: An Ever-Expanding Universe* 68
    6.2 *Transmedia Practices Extended from Collins's Novels* 70
    6.3 *The Work of Religion/Art and* The Hunger Games *Transmedia Assemblage* 72
  Bibliography 78

Religion and the Arts in *The Hunger Games*

Zhange Ni
Virginia Tech, Blacksburg, Virginia, USA
nizhange@vt.edu

Abstract

In this selective overview of scholarship generated by *The Hunger Games*—the young adult dystopian fiction and film series which has won popular and critical acclaim—Zhange Ni showcases various investigations into the entanglement of religion and the arts in the new millennium. Ni introduces theories, methods, and the latest developments in the study of religion in relation to state politics, audio/visual art, material culture, reality TV, and transmedia projects, whilst also reading *The Hunger Games* as a story that explores the variety, complexity, and ambiguity of enchantment. In popular texts such as *The Hunger Games*, religion and art—both broadly construed, that is, beyond conventional boundaries—converge in creating an enchantment that makes life more bearable and effects change in the world.

Keywords

The Hunger Games – religion and the arts – enchantment – ritual sacrifice – sovereign power – folk music – painting – material objects – reality TV – food – clothing – transmedia storytelling

1   Introduction

Suzanne Collins's (1962–) *The Hunger Games* trilogy—*The Hunger Games* (2008), *Catching Fire* (2009), and *Mockingjay* (2010)—is a commercially successful and critically acclaimed young adult dystopian series. It has been adapted by Lionsgate into four films: *The Hunger Games* (2012), *The Hunger Games: Catching Fire* (2013), *The Hunger Games: Mockingjay—Part 1* (2014), and *The Hunger Games: Mockingjay—Part 2* (2015). These novels and films, together with their extensions into other commercial projects and a whole variety of fan cultures, have generated a considerable amount of academic discussion in the second decade of the twenty-first century.

This article provides an overview of current scholarship that discusses religion and the arts in *The Hunger Games* universe—that is, the novels, films, and transmedia practices centered upon them. By no means an exhaustive survey of all the articles and books devoted to this textual universe, this study fixates its attention on two entangled topics: religion and the arts. It is to be highlighted at the outset that this article does not adopt the modern, Western, and Protestant model of religion as interiorized, privatized, and depoliticized piety in some transcendent existence. Instead, it takes religion as embodied practices in which humans interact with the material world, of which they are an integral aspect. This world is infused with forces not necessarily acknowledged in the scientific, rationalistic worldview of the post-Enlightenment West. Correspondingly, the concept of art here is broadly construed. It is not restricted to fine art primarily concerned with beauty and aesthetics and instead encompasses ritual performance, material culture, and mass entertainment, to name just a few.

I have chosen to showcase research perspectives in the study of religion and the arts by surveying scholarship on *The Hunger Games* universe for two reasons. First, the novels/films are a window open onto the real-life world in the early twenty-first century. The dystopian imaginary of these novels/films is rooted in real-world issues such as the expansion of state power, the domination of global capitalism, and the abuse of science and technology. In the fictional space of *The Hunger Games* as well as in our world that has given rise to this fiction, both religion and art are going through radical transformations. This calls for scholarly investigations into the new configurations of both categories as encapsulated in these popular texts, while the discussions reviewed in this article have already laid a foundation for, or made attempts at, such investigations. Second, existing scholarly articles and books on *The Hunger Games* universe were produced in the second decade of the twenty-first century. Critically examining these analyses, which represent recent trends and innovations in multiple fields, I introduce the theories developed, methods deployed, and questions raised in these fields to scholars and students interested in the study of religion and the arts.

This review article is organized around the theme of enchantment, the work that religion and art share in common to transform (our perception of) something into something else with the hope of helping the enchanted to cope with existential difficulties. *The Hunger Games* novels/films tell a story of various types of enchantment, some of which are always in contestation. Before offering a synopsis of these novels/films, I turn to three scholars who have considered the entanglement of religion and art in enchantment—namely, Michael Jackson, David Morgan, and David Chidester.

Jackson, an anthropologist of religion, argues in *The Work of Art: Rethinking the Elementary Forms of Religious Life* (2016) that religion and art imply each other, because they are both human responses to existential situations in which "material impoverishment, social injustice, and psychic wounds undermine our capacity to live as we wish" (2016: 2). What is his idea of religion? What does he talk about when he talks about art? With regard to religion, Jackson questions Émile Durkheim's (1858–1917) definition as proposed in *Elementary Forms of Religious Life* ([1912]1995). Durkheim explained religion as the collective ideas and practices that shape the moral universe of a given society and made a distinction between the sacred and the profane, the former standing at the center of community formation, apart from the rhythms of everyday life, and the latter associated with the utilitarian activities of various individuals. According to Durkheim, religion is primarily a matter of the sacred. Accusing Durkheim of sociological reductionism, Jackson seeks to identify the building blocks of religious experience by paying attention to "the various ways in which collective representations are taken up, glossed, or acted upon by individuals in everyday situations" (2016: 9). That is to say, the distinction of the sacred and the profane is more porous than fixed.

Jackson is also dissatisfied with the Protestant model of religion, one that is focused on faith, liturgy, authoritative texts, and established institutions. Instead, he prefers to take religion "as mystics might understand it—something one discovers for oneself through direct experience, and articulates in one's own way" (2016: 14). This process of discovery is meant to help the individual "gain some purchase on shattering experiences and regain some measure of comprehension and control over their lives" (Jackson 2016: xv). However, his "mystical" religion does not break away from the Protestant model because it is still centered upon the individual. While Durkheim overlooked how individuals process collective representations in the realm of the profane, what is downplayed in Jackson's conceptualization is the building of community and solidarity in the experience and expression of various individuals.

When it comes to art, Jackson calls for a more flexible understanding. He abolishes the distinction between art as self-expression and craft as the production of something tangible and practical. Furthermore, the study of art does not need to focus exclusively on an artist (her experience or its expression) or an art object (its aesthetic properties, market value, or social acceptability). What interests Jackson is the work of art—that is, "a way of processing experience and working it through" (2016: xiv), a technique "inextricably connected to storytelling, play, dreaming, and ritual, whereby we work out vital relationships between inner desires and external determinants" (2016: 3). Given the intimate entanglement of religion and art, what the elementary forms of religious experience do is the work of art.

For Jackson, religion and art share the same creative processes that serve as coping mechanisms or defensive strategies that protect us from the very reality that has become too much to manage by any conventional means. These shared creative processes are able to open up what he calls "the third space." Jackson describes this artificial space as one in which we try to "get around or beyond the mundane difficulties that beset us and the misfortunes that befall us" (2016: xiv). In this space, we try to remake the world, or at least reconfigure our sense of being-in-the-world, by "acting upon the world to the same extent that it acts upon itself—a process of converting what is given into what is chosen and transforming what was not one's own making into an assemblage over which one asserts mastery" (Jackson 2016: 32).

Earlier I pointed out that Jackson centers on the individual while reconsidering religion. Moreover, this individual only pursues self-mastery, although more often than not in an illusory sense. What I endeavor to demonstrate in this article, by taking a critical look at the existing scholarship on *The Hunger Games* universe and developing my own interpretation of the text, is that religious/artistic experience belongs to both the individual and the collective, with the two being mutually constitutive. And, religion and art perform the work of *both* self-empowerment *and* self-abandonment.

Morgan, a scholar of religion and an art historian, sees religion, art, and other similar human endeavors as nonrational work undertaken toward making a home in the universe that does not have to be friendly or hospitable to the human beings. In his book *Images at Work: The Material Culture of Enchantment* (2018), he calls this type of nonrational work—or, the interplay of the interior and exterior to create the third space—enchantment. Religion and art are inseparable because enchantment is at work in both. Morgan emphasizes that there are two types of enchantment. The first type, what Jackson means by the elementary forms of religion or the work of art, focuses on "the subject, empowering him or her to bend reality in some way to accommodate one's desire." The second type "emanates from an object's or image's power over someone" (Morgan 2018: 4).

Although Jackson does recognize that the external world acts upon us, he only deals with the first type of enchantment that consists of what we do to the world to avoid or achieve an outcome that we have no independent power to affect, and to create an illusion of mastery for the human subject. By contrast,

Morgan is more interested in the power within things and what images do to us. He highlights that "enchantment involves a structure or framework of action that surpasses one's sphere of power" (2018: 18) and that this structure/framework is activated by material objects, sounds, and sensations. Agency is also grounded in nonhuman things, or, more precisely, an assemblage of things human and nonhuman "whose webbed relations are accessed and activated by images" (Morgan 2018: 169). As humans organize their experience, human experience is also arranged by images within these human-nonhuman relations. Enchantment is *both* self-empowerment *and* the willing submission of the self to the (non)human other. The ultimate goal of enchantment is to make a home in the universe. "One mends its ruptures, extends its reach, and daily repeats its assuring routines. The world takes shape as a result and shapes its inhabitants in return. The home that arises is a sense of belonging, the feeling that a place has been made for us and will reward our labors at survival and improvement" (Morgan 2018: 170).

It is worth noting that Morgan discusses the politics of enchantment, acknowledging that enchantment—that is, both types of enchantment—may serve the interests of particular individuals, classes, and nations, that it always comes at someone's gain and another's loss, and that there is fierce competition between different enchantments and a constant need for dis-enchantment and re-enchantment. In other words, the self-empowering and home-making efforts by some may be a destructive force for others. This is why attempts at self-emptying or the embrace of homelessness, a theme Morgan is not concerned with, may also be a means for human survival and flourishing. The annihilation of the self in the face of and for the sake of the other, something neither Jackson nor Morgan pays attention to, is to be considered in our reading of *The Hunger Games*.

Chidester, an expert of comparative religion, also discusses the politics of enchantment, although he does not use the term explicitly. In *Religion: Material Dynamics* (2018), Chidester argues that religion is always already situated at the intersection of multiple domains, while the sacred is not monopolized by what may be readily identified as religion, because "anything can be sacralized through the ... work of intensive interpretation, regular ritualization, and inevitable contestation over ownership of the means, modes, and forces for producing the sacred" (2018: 30). What he suggests, echoing Jackson and Morgan, is that religion is not a realm set apart from everyday life but "flows through popular culture, social networks, political mobilizations, economic transactions, and other configurations" (2018: 8).

Resonating with Jackson's idea of the third space and Morgan's make-shift home, Chidester talks about the role of religion—and art by extension—as signaling "a terrain in which human beings engage in meaningful and powerful ways with the material constraints and animations of matter, the interplay of sacralizing and desecrating, the labor of producing space and time, and the myriad ways in which incongruity, the material effect of the collision of incommensurables, can be transposed into moments, perhaps fleeting moments, of congruence" (2018: 2–3). For Chidester, religion and art are intricately implicated, both mediations at the intersection of personal subjectivity, social collectivities, and the world beyond human control.

Compared with Morgan who is fascinated with material objects, Chidester takes a step further by explaining the two senses of materiality in relation to religion/art. The first material, one that Morgan is primarily concerned with, refers to "the stuff of religion, the bodies, objects, and places of religious life that are animated through practices of sensory engagement, economic exchange, and technological mediation" (Chidester 2018: 79). The second material involves the material conditions of capitalism, colonialism, and imperialism and the material consequences of circulating humans, things, and practices. These conditions and consequences make materiality matter in religion, while "religion is something, if it is anything, that moves from embodied intimacy to global economy in material circulations" (Chidester 2018: 10).

The enchantment of religion and art makes the sacred in individual and collective lives to protect us, although not always all of us, against the onslaughts of unbearable hardships. This enchantment is to be examined in the framework of historical materialism, or, more specifically, in the historical material conditions for and consequences of human attempts to negotiate the human-(non)human relationships within the networks of human-nonhuman things. Enchantment, whether self-empowering or self-abandoning, is a double-edged sword, repressive and liberatory at the same time, depending on who reaps the benefit and who pays the price. And, enchantment, the work of religion/art, is a key theme of *The Hunger Games*, as this article will illustrate and analyze.

The setting of the novels/films is America in the distant future. After our world has been destroyed by a series of natural disasters, a regime named Panem rules today's North America, which is divided into the Capitol and thirteen Districts. A civil war breaks out between the privileged Capitol and the disenfranchised Districts, resulting in the obliteration of District 13 and the suppression of the other twelve Districts. From then on, the Capitol begins to stage the annual Hunger Game, forcing each District to turn in two tributes—two children between the ages of twelve and eighteen—and make them fight against one another within an arena until the sole survivor walks away to become a national celebrity, as the Hunger Game is broadcast live on TV. It is no exaggeration to say that Panem evolves around *The Hunger Games* reality show, which entertains the Capitol, terrorizes the Districts, and disciplines everyday life all over the country.

The protagonist of the novels/films, Katniss Everdeen, is a girl of sixteen at the beginning of the story and one of the two tributes from District 12 to participate in the 74th Hunger Game. It is originally her younger sister Primrose who gets selected as a tribute in the reaping process. But to protect Prim, Katniss volunteers to take her place and enters the arena with Peeta Mellark, another child from the same District. Although the Capitol pits all of the children in the arena against one another, Katniss makes friends with Rue, a girl from District 11, and forms an alliance with Peeta, who is secretly in love with her. The first novel ends with Katniss and Peeta attempting to commit double suicide to deprive the game of its sole survivor. Thrilled by this romantic ending, the gamemakers and the audiences want both of them to survive. As a result, for the first time, *The Hunger Games* show allows a pair of survivors.

In the second novel, President Coriolanus Snow, unhappy about the defiance of Katniss and Peeta, throws them into the Quarter Quell, the 75th Hunger Game in which winners from the previous years must fight again. Meanwhile, another rebellion of the Districts against the Capitol is about to break out. The rebels manage to save some tributes, including Katniss, from the arena. The third novel unfolds during the second civil war. Katniss becomes the face of the resistance force led by District 13, which has gone underground and reemerges as the organizing center of the second rebellion. Toward the end of the novel, the rebels succeed in bringing down the reign of the Capitol and of President Snow in particular. However, noticing that District 13 is becoming another Capitol, Katniss assassinates their leader, President Coin. In the epilogue of the trilogy, the reader meets Katniss as a middle-aged woman married to Peeta with two kids. With the nightmare of the games and the war over, she watches her children playing in the field, where the dead are buried.

In my engagement with the scholarship devoted to *The Hunger Games*—the novels, films, and other transmedia projects—I pay particular attention to the repressive enchantment of the Hunger Games, and the liberatory enchantment enacted by the protagonist and her friends. On the one hand, the annual Hunger Game is a state ritual that creates the collective identity of Panem, sacralizes its political, economic, and technological order, and assists the Capitol in overcoming its misfortunes—the natural disasters that annihilated the civilization predating Panem and the rebellion of the Districts that once destabilized the established regime. On the other hand, the repressed people resort to singing, painting, and other religious/artistic work to put up their tiny resistance, which is also a third space where the world could go their way. In this space, the enchantment of Panem's totalitarian politics and consumerist economy is the cause of the "material impoverishment, social injustice, and psychic wounds" (Jackson 2016:2) of the disenfranchised, who yearn for justice and freedom and seek disenchantment and re-enchantment.

The repressive enchantment of Panem and the liberatory enchantment of the young tributes are intertwined in not only the Hunger Games of Panem but also a) *The Hunger Games* show that mediates the fight within the arena and the everyday life outside of it, b) the game of hungers over food and clothing inside the fictional space, and c) the tug-of-war between the capture of capitalism and the irruption of grassroots creativity over the transmedia assemblage of *The Hunger Games*. In this light, I consider the show, the game of hungers, and the transmedia assemblage as instances of split enchantment, both repressive and liberatory. I then argue that a) *The Hunger Games* reality TV show is the state religion/art of Panem, b) the game of hungers centered upon daily sustenance is the lived religion or everyday art of the Capitol and the Districts, and c) *The Hunger Games* transmedia assemblage encapsulates the extension of the contested enchantments from the imaginary realm into the real-life world.

The five sections following this introduction study the variety of enchantments named above: ritual sacrifice as controlled by the Capitol; the resistance of everyday religious/artistic practices; the enchantment of *The Hunger Games* reality show as split between the repressive power of Panem and the resistance of the powerless; the split enchantment of food and clothing beyond the game arenas and TV screens; and the split enchantment of transmedia storytelling as exemplified by *The Hunger Games* universe. In addition to presenting scholarship that sheds light on all these enchantments in the text and highlighting the theories and methods deployed in these analyses, I will provide my critical assessment of these books and articles, offer my own interpretation of the novels/films, and comment on the scholarly paradigms and research perspectives in the study of religion and the arts.

2   Enchantment 1: Sovereign Power and Ritual Sacrifice

The fictional world of *The Hunger Games* series is centered upon the Hunger Games. Panem, a sovereign power that controls life and death, stages the annual game, a sacrificial ritual that performs the dark enchantment of politics, economy, and technoscience. In this section, I begin with summarizing scholarship that researches the extratextual models of Panem and reads Panem in light of Michel Foucault (1926–1984) and Giorgio Agamben (1942–) who theorized sovereign power. Next, I focus on articles analyzing ritual sacrifice in the novels/films with reference to René Girard (1923–2015), Georges Bataille (1897–1962), and Theodor Adorno (1903–1969) and Max Horkheimer (1895–1973). Last but not the least, scholars of *The Hunger Games* have also examined self-sacrifice for the sake of the other, invoking Emmanuel Levinas (1906–1995) and Jacques Derrida (1930–2004).

On the basis of existing scholarly discussion, I argue that the annual game, a form of ritual sacrifice, does the enchanting work to create the sacred, the core ideologies and practices of Panem—authoritarian politics, neoliberal economy, and science and technology in service to the former two. The agenda of the Hunger Games is to turn Panem into a new deity, whose sovereign power governs the life and death of its subjects. However, another sacrifice is possible. In liberatory enchantment, the other to which the self willingly submits is not the sovereign power of Panem but the other powerless individuals and communities. It is to be added that the sacred also exists as the loving bond among the sacrificed, who place the other above themselves and dare to rise up against Panem.

2.1   *Inventing Panem: Sovereign Power and Bare Life*

The making of Panem is a major topic in *The Hunger Games* scholarship. Collins took inspiration from the Greek and Roman legacy, dystopian literature in the twentieth century, contemporary American politics and culture, and capitalist expansion on a global scale. First of all, her trilogy is indebted to the repository of Greek mythology. Scholars have highlighted the correspondences between Katniss and various mythic figures such as Theseus (the prince of Athens who volunteered as a tribute to fight the monster of Crete), Artemis (a virgin goddess, hunter, and archer), and Philomela (a woman seeking revenge and associated with the bird nightingale). It has been noted that the Capitol of Panem and its Districts are reincarnations of Crete and Athens in the myth of Theseus, with Crete (Capitol) having conquered Athens (Districts), demanding children from the latter and sacrificing them to punish the defeated.[1]

Panem is also Collins's reimagination of the Roman Empire.[2] The very name of Panem is taken from the famous phrase "*panem et cirsenses*" (bread and circuses) by the satirist Juvenal, referring to the ruling strategy of

---

1 For articles that study how Collins drew on Greek mythology, see Mills 2015; Hansen 2015; Salman-Mitchell and Alvares 2018.
2 For articles that shed light on the connections between the Roman Empire and Collins's Panem, see Aitchison 2015; Heit 2015; Makins 2015; Soncini 2015.

controlling people by focusing their attention on food and entertainment and away from civic responsibilities and political self-determination. According to Marian Makins, the political geography and economic structure of Panem replicates the historical situation of the Roman Empire, which consisted of a metropolis and its surrounding provinces, with the former relying on importations from the provinces, each associated with the specific goods it produced (2015).

Makins also points out that Panem differs from the historical Roman Empire "in the degree of control exerted by the imperial authority" (2015: 286). Furthermore, the conception of Rome as a totalitarian state characterized by might and vice is not supported by archeological or other "hard" evidence but invented by ancient literature—"the exaggerated satirical tableaux of Horace, Juvenal, and Petronius; the sensationalized Imperial portraiture of Suetonius and Tacitus; the philosophical moralizing of Seneca; the ascetic treatises of Christian apologist Tertullian" (Makins 2015: 287). What inspired Collins is not so much the historical Rome as Hollywood's Roman epics produced during the Cold War, such as *Quo Vadis* (1951), *Ben-Hur* (1959), and *Spartacus* (1960), films "present[ing] the Empire as a parallel to a modern totalitarian regime like Nazi Germany or the Soviet Union ...[and] pillory[ing] a repressive element within American society" (Makins 2015: 284).

Collins's Panem, a transfiguration of the fictional Rome, is built upon another pre-existing and long-standing fiction, dystopia. Scholars have associated Collins's novels with classical dystopian texts such as Aldous Huxley's *Brave New World* (1932), George Orwell's *1984* (1949), Ray Bradbury's *Fahrenheit 451* (1953), William Golding's *Lord of the Flies* (1954), and more recent texts such as Stephen King's *Running Man* (1982) and the Japanese film *Battle Royale* directed by Kinji Fukasaku (2000) (Martin 2014; Trites 2014). Moreover, the term "dystopian," although unquestionably loaded with a Cold War anxiety and often used to attack communism and socialism, also refers to what is repressive in contemporary America. Revisiting the Roman gladiator paradigm, David Aitchison reads Howard Fast's *Spartacus* (1951), on which Kubric and Douglas's film *Spartacus* (1960) was based, as a "sympathetic lament for the failed communist revolution" (2015: 254). That is to say, the Roman Empire in Collins's favorite movie could be interpreted as the capitalist system instead of the totalitarian Communist government.

Panem is undeniably America. Makins discusses the dystopian reality of media desensitization—the mindless consumption of violent media—as a feature of contemporary American culture (2015). Andrea Ruthven critiques the American dystopia of rampant consumerism (2017). Angela Hubler demonstrates that the fictional Panem (not just the Capitol but also, more significantly, the Districts) is not without its material base in the United States, where the poverty rate for children has risen as "a consequence of the current economic crisis, itself the culmination of long-term trends" that have "filled the pockets of international finance capitalists" and left the working class struggling with increasing debt (2014: 237–8).

The internally divided America is representative of global capitalism. Bill Clemente argues that "Panem operates not so much like the Imperial Roman government … but more like a modern global conglomerate" (2012: 24), with the Capitol (representing capitalist corporations) taking advantage of the crisis of the rebellion to "privat[ize] government functions and exploit wealth to the disadvantage of the majority" (2012: 25). Similarly, studying the film adaptation of *The Hunger Games* (2012), Mark Fisher suggests that Panem is what Michael Hardt and Antonio Negri have called Empire, a new type of sovereignty beyond the nation-state, against which Multitude, a new political subject, is flickering into existence (2012).

As illustrated above, Panem is a mutation of multiple sources—the Greek and Roman legacy, the history of totalitarian regimes, and the reality of contemporary America and beyond. Correspondingly, Panem's absolute power over life and death is a fusion of premodern sovereign power and modern biopolitics as conceptualized by Foucault and Agamben, two theorists frequently quoted in discussions of politics in *The Hunger Games*.[3] In *Discipline and Punish* ([1979]1995), Foucault studied the historical transition from sovereign power to disciplinary power. The term sovereign power refers to the absolute power that a monarch wields over his or her subjects and their behavior. Prior to the eighteenth century, sovereign power was mainly exercised through public torture and executions. These practices were designed to create a spectacle, the goal of which was to evoke the feelings of terror in the audience, who were required to be present for the public ritual and learn that any future offence would be likewise punished. In this light, the deadly games, the public torture and executions of children from the Districts, are meant to terrorize the audiences of the Districts. Sovereign power in a premodern sense is at work.

Foucault also proposed the idea of disciplinary power. Around the seventeenth and eighteenth centuries, new modalities of power began to emerge. In the early nineteenth century, modern governments were no longer comfortable

---

3   Kelley Wezner, Sean P. Connors, and Michael Macaluso and Cori Mckenzie have all examined the sovereign and disciplinary power of Panem, paying particular attention to the various panoptions in the novels/films. Invoking Foucault, Christina van Dyke has studied the disciplinary power of fashion, while Fani Cettl uses Agamben to discuss the biopolitics of reality TV. See Wezner 2012; Connors 2014a, b; Macaluso and Mckenzie 2014; van Dyke 2012; Cettl 2015.

with the public display of barbarism and began to discipline their subjects. Sovereign power gave way to disciplinary power, which, instead of torturing the body, relies on a set of social institutions—prisons, hospitals, schools, and factories, to name a few—and authorities of knowledge to discipline the "soul" (subjectivity) of the individual.

Foucault borrowed the image of the panopticon from Jeremy Bentham (1748–1832) to illustrate how disciplinary power works. The panopticon is a circular structure with a guard tower located at its center, from where guards watch over the prisoners. Under constant surveillance, the prisoners internalize the gaze of the guards and discipline themselves accordingly. In other words, within a panopticon, the modern subject learns to internalize certain rules and regulate themselves. Meanwhile, sovereign power transforms into the laws upheld and enforced by modern institutions such as the police and the judicial system. In contrast to the old sovereign power and the new legal system that still punishes the subjects when they break the laws, disciplinary power holds the individuals responsible for exercising power over themselves and conforming to behavioral norms. What disciplinary power produces is docile bodies, the objects of power and instruments of its exercise at the same time. These bodies are what Panem desires in its citizens, both in the Capitol and the Districts.

In addition to disciplinary power, Foucault developed the idea of biopower, a technology and apparatus of power aimed at governing a population's life forces. In "Security, Territory, and Population," he used the term biopolitics to refer to "the endeavor … to rationalize the problems presented to governmental practice by the phenomena characteristic of a group of living human beings constituted as a population" since the eighteenth century (1997: 73). While disciplinary power produces individual docile bodies, biopolitics manages entire populations. Through biopolitics, the modern state actively intervenes in the life of the people, taking care of their health, hygiene, and reproduction to sustain and expand the human base of state power. This is precisely the goal to be accomplished by the Hunger Games (the fight within the arenas) and *The Hunger Games* show (broadcast to the entire nation).

Foucault contrasted biopolitics with the thanapolitics of the old sovereign power, the former concerned with improving lives, the latter a power to kill. However, the old sovereign power and the new disciplinary power and biopower are still entangled because the cultivation of a better life is inseparable from the more efficient authorization of a holocaust. Building on Foucault, Giorgio Agamben argues in *Homo Sacer: Sovereign Power and Bare Life* (1998) that the sovereign power to kill is still at work in modern biopolitics. Biopolitics and thanapolitics are two sides of the same coin. Agamben introduces the term "bare life" to illuminate the relation between the sovereign power to kill and the living subject. Originally the figure of *homo sacer* in Roman law—a body expelled from the Roman city and ready to be killed by anyone without committing a crime—bare life in the modern world exists as the flip side of the concept of the human as instituted in ideas such as human rights and dwells within the body of every citizen of the nation-state. He sees the Nazi concentration camp as the very paradigm for modern biopolitics and the production of bare life. There is always a fracture between the people managed by any nation-state—not just the Nazi regime—and various "inferior" bodies always ready to be expended for the sake of unity.

According to Agamben, bare life is produced through three paradoxical pairs of relations: inclusion and exclusion, exception and norm, and bio and zoe. The Nazis built the concentration camp to contain bare life, which could not be tolerated within the city. Hence, bare life was included through its exclusion. The camp was established as a state of exception that later became a normal situation. The camp was the dumping place for those bodies marked as less than human (bio) and closer to animal and natural life (zoe). The game arena in *The Hunger Games* novels/films replicates the Nazi camp, whereas the tributes reaped into the games exemplify bare life. Every year, a new arena is built somewhere in the vicinity of the Capitol to house the game. This arena is the very heart of life in Panem in that the cut-throat competition between the tributes is broadcast to the entire nation to cultivate a particular lifestyle. The tributes, young adults from the districts and the working classes, once selected by a lottery system, are banished from ordinary life and rendered killable to each other inside the arena, a state of exception for the Hobbesian total war. They, perceived as less valuable lives in the first place, fall further from being fully human, their bodies becoming indistinguishable from animals and muttants. This exceptional state sets up the normative paradigm for the biopolitics of Panem, one that produces bare life and promotes better life, two sides of the same coin, concurrently.

Having introduced theories of sovereign power, I take a closer look at Panem, a godless world that has itself become a new deity. The high-tech arena, a self-enclosed mini-world, makes possible Panem's omnipotent power, which goes beyond the political and natural law to demand sacrifice. The ruling class located in the Capitol are beyond the political law. They are exempted from the game, which draws only from the Districts. Citizens of the Capitol enter the arena only after the game, as tourists seeking entertainment. And, although the trilogy is devoid of magic and supernatural power, Panem transcends the natural law inside the arena, which is full of deadly special effects. Gamemakers in the control room create inclement weather and monster-mutations to make the tributes' fight more difficult, and thus more exciting to the audience. When gamemakers play with computer simulation and genetic engineering, they help to turn Panem into God.

What Hobbes meant by the "natural condition of man" is replicated in the artificially constructed and remotely controlled arena. The fight inside the arena is clearly his "total war" of everyone against everyone else. However, in the trilogy, the "natural" condition is not just a human construct but a state project. Panem reverses the conceptualization of Leviathan. According to Hobbes, it is the commonwealth, or the more well-known Leviathan, that comes into being as a result of the social contract and that steps in to end the natural condition or the total war by appropriating and monopolizing violence (2005). To the contrary, Panem acknowledges its origin in a civil war and perpetuates its foundational violence by manufacturing the natural condition and staging the total war inside the arena. The arena is the norm of Panem's political configuration. That is to say, the entirety of Panem is an arena, where the fight to the death inside the small arenas, the hand-to-mouth labor of the Districts, and the endless consumption of the Capitol are all interconnected.

Panem controls not only its people and other life forms—including bioengineered creatures within and beyond the game arenas[4]—but also historiography and geography.[5] It claims to be omnipresent, a cosmic presence. It is to be noted that the fictional universe of the text is absent of any country other than Panem and void of any prehistory before the Dark Days of the first civil war. The bio-spatial-temporal totality of Panem is produced by a whole series of pre- and post-arena events, beginning with the national reaping and culminating in the national victory tour. The calendar year of Panem is divided into the game season and the waiting period. The cyclical game is a regeneration ritual that ensures the "eternal return" of Panem, to borrow the term from Mircea Eliade.

Reaping marks the beginning of the game season and constitutes Panem's population census (essentially, a biopolitical mechanism). Everyone must attend the ceremony in a public square, with children between twelve and eighteen forming several rows, their name cards placed inside two glass balls (for the two genders). The state power of Panem reaches every individual in the Districts, marks them by age, and picks the tributes in the name of fate.

---

4 For discussion of humans, animals, and human-animal hybrids, all manipulated by Panem's science and technology, as well as the potentials of going beyond a fixed human identity, see King 2012; Eberl 2012; Smyth 2014; Connors 2014a; Guanio-Uluru 2017.

5 For discussion of how Panem controls time and space, with history and memory on the one hand and landscape (natural and/or artificial—the distinction between the two always blurred) on the other, see Koenig 2012; Baker 2014; Connors 2014a; Krikowa 2018.

However, fate is actually the sovereign power of Panem that pretends to be the whimsical will of the cosmos. While fate picks the tributes, the entire population is in the grip of Panem.

The reaping process continues when tributes take the bullet train to the Capitol and then, wearing glamorous makeup and outfits, ride chariots into the training center. This parade of tributes and chariots, resembling the parade of the nations in the opening ceremony of the modern Olympic games, is meant to display the main industry and cultural identity of each District and the unification of all these Districts and the Capitol into Panem. This parade is also a demonic parody of the Senate, because the Districts, which the tributes represent, are united into Panem, like the United States of America.

The United Districts of Panem emerge from the fight in the arena. The only survivor becomes the ultimate representative of the twenty-four tributes representing the twelve Districts. He or she represents the unified identity of Panem. The reversal of the pre-arena train ride and chariot parade is the post-arena victory tour. The ultimate representative travels from the Capitol, all the way through the twelve Districts, then back to his or her crowning ceremony in the Capitol. Although Panem has an air force, tributes always take the train. The railway system is the blood vein of Panem's national/geographical body. The railway takes tributes and goods from the twelve Districts to the Capitol, and victors and soldiers (ironically called Peacekeepers) from the Capitol to the Districts. During the final tour, the victor/survivor has to chant this slogan wherever he or she visits: "Panem today. Panem tomorrow. Panem forever." Not only the entire population and landscape but also time is reaped by the omnipresent Panem.

Panem is panentheistic, meaning that God penetrates the world but transcends it as well. Panem both reaps and exists beyond its people, land, and history. To maintain absolute control, it has to see all from above. The structuring principle of the theologico-political requires a site of perfect vision; political/theological sovereignty requires omniscience. The arena where Panem exercises its omnipotence must be camera-saturated. It must become a panopticon. Covered by cameras for surveillance and entertainment, the Eye of Panem never blinks—either in or outside the arena. What connects the arena and the entire territory of Panem is not just the train ride back and forth but also, in an even more effective way, the television, an omniscient network of camera eyes and TV screens. Like participation in the national reaping, watching *The Hunger Games* show is compulsory. Everyone sees through the Eye of Panem, which sees everyone seeing. The essence of television is that the eye of the camera and the eyes of the spectator are distinct and that the viewers see something from a point of view other than their own. There is thus a radical asymmetry between viewers and the camera. The eyes of the viewers are not allowed to look back at the Eye of Panem, although they must always look through that Eye to be enchanted by the religious/artistic work of the sacrificial game.

2.2 *Creating the Sacred through Ritual Sacrifice*

In her interview with James Blasingame, Collins named the Greek myth of Theseus, the hero who subdued the monster Minotaur, and the story of Spartacus, the slave-gladiator who rebelled against the Roman Empire, as the two prototypes for Katniss. What the Theseus myth and the gladiator paradigm share in common is the theme of sacrifice as a means of political domination. In Greek mythology, King Minos of Crete defeated Athens and forced the Athenians to send seven boys and seven girls every nine years to be devoured by the Minotaur, a monster lurking in a gigantic labyrinth. Theseus, the young prince of Athens, volunteered as one of the tributes to kill the monster (Plutarch's *Life of Theseus* 17.2). Collins remarked that she had "appropriated the Greek mythological premise of a conquering power that bent all of its subjects to its will through violence and maintained fear and domination through a not so subtle reminder to the neighboring peoples that they are not free and autonomous" (Blasingame 2007: 727). In her novels, "Crete" is the Capitol, which conquered "Athens," the rebelling Districts, and made them pay "tributes," twenty-four young children, every year. Resembling Theseus, Katniss volunteers to take the place of Primrose to fight in the fatal game. In doing so, she becomes the unexpected reincarnation of not just Theseus but also Spartacus in a teenage girl.

Regarding Katniss's Roman predecessor, Collins claimed that she had "researched not only the historical Spartacus and the popular media about him, but many of the historical gladiators from pre-Christian times … and … found three things always present in the gladiator paradigm: (1) a ruthless government that (2) forces people to fight to the death and (3) uses these fights to the death as a form of popular entertainment" (Blasingame 2007: 727). Breaking out of the coliseum, Spartacus led a rebellion against Rome (Plutarch's *Life of Crassus* 8.1–11.8), while Katniss joins the second rebellion against the Capitol. Unlike Spartacus who was captured and executed, Katniss survives and eventually helps to bring down the "ruthless government" of Panem.

Both tributes and gladiators are sacrificial victims. And, the labyrinth in the story of Theseus and the Roman Coliseum for gladiatorial combat merge into the arenas where the Hunger Games are fought. While Sophie Mills reads the Muttants, human-animal hybrids created by the gamemakers to torture tributes, as a modern transfiguration of the Minotaur (2015: 56), I see Panem as the ultimate Minotaur. The real monster is the sovereign power of Crete that demanded the tributes, Rome that made gladiators fight each other, and the fictional Panem that stages the Hunger Games as state-sponsored ritual sacrifice. French sociologists in the late nineteenth and early twentieth centuries regarded sacrifice as an opportunity to communicate with the divine (Hubert and Mauss 1981) or, to bring up Durkheim again, to create and maintain the sacred.

An elementary religious/artistic form that generates enchantment to empower some at the expense of the others, the Hunger Games constitute the third space, the make-shift home, or the terrain where incongruities transform into congruence discussed in the introductory section. What happens within this space/home/terrain is sacrifice. Among scholars wrestling with the multifarious phenomenon of sacrifice in the *Hunger Games* novels and films, Jeffrey Williams (2018), Emily McAvan (2017), and Bruce Martin (2014) are worthy of particular attention. For them, the function of sacrifice is to build a political order through the infliction of violence upon a few for the greater good, to squander society's excess in the hope of keeping the economy running by promoting competition and consumption, and to establish and maintain the hegemony of science and technology, indispensable instruments for the dominant political economy. In short, the sacred brought into being by the Hunger Games is the political, economic, and technoscientific order of Panem.

First of all, the ritual sacrifice of the Hunger Games makes Panem the political community sacred. In this regard, both Williams and McAvan invoke Girard. Working along the line of the French sociological tradition introduced earlier, Girard theorized sacrifice in *Violence and the Sacred* (1977) and *The Scapegoat* (1986). Acknowledging that sacrifice is communion with the sacred, he pointed out that violence is central in this communion. For him, ritualized violence is a regulating mechanism that resolves the rivalries and conflicts within a community by redirecting communal hostilities towards a scapegoat, who is allegedly guilty. Tension always exists in a community, as its members, although assigned to different social positions, desire the same object and threaten to fight over it. In the novels/films, this fight broke out more than seventy-four years before the story starts, when the Districts rebelled against the Capitol, with both sides desiring the same object, limited natural resources and human products. The Districts were defeated. As punishment, the Capitol started to demand two children from each District every year and have them fight against one another to the death. The annual Hunger Game is more than public punishment and executions to intimidate the Districts. It is ritual sacrifice that releases the tension between the Capitol and the Districts by designating and destroying the scapegoat.

For Girard, the scapegoat—most likely slaves, livestock, and children—comes from neither the outside nor the inside. The sacrificial victim is both inside and outside, same as and different from, the community that sacrifices her. Her killing is a "good" form of violence, because it is a small price paid to stave off the "bad" violence of larger-scale conflict or war. Girard contended that this ritual substitution of "good" violence for the "bad" is a feature of "primitive" societies, whereas modern societies have replaced sacrifice with the justice of the legal system. In this light, Williams compares the Hunger Games with child sacrifice in the biblical tradition and broader ancient Near Eastern cultures—the offering of children to a god or gods to consolidate the foundation of a civic community or to protect it from some impending disaster. However, the political community of Panem, a god-like entity that demands sacrifice, is not "primitive" but a projection of our modern and contemporary world.

The Hunger Games are also neoliberal games that sacralize the economic order, an order in which market principles have infiltrated various, if not all, aspects of individual life and socio-political spheres. Acknowledging this, McAvan turns to Bataille, who linked sacrifice, together with orgy and war, to the expenditure of the excess that society has produced and which cannot be completely absorbed in its growth. In *The Accursed Share* (1988), Bataille demonstrated that this excess is better willingly and gloriously spent in order to avoid some unwilling catastrophes. The wasting of this extra energy is luxurious—that is, beyond the rational calculations determined by limited resources and aimed at future gains. It is in such luxury that the Capitol, an affluent society built upon the exploitation of the Districts, indulges. In McAvan's reading, the tributes are luxurious items for the Capitol dwellers, not unlike gourmet food and exuberant clothing. These young children are the valuable human resources of the Districts to be squandered by the Capitol. The Hunger Games are by necessity the most spectacular party of all parties and the foundation of a consumerist society.

According to Girard, the sacrificial victims are scapegoats with less, if not little, value, which is why the community can afford to sacrifice them. By contrast, Bataille saw excessive value in them and the expenditure of this value in their sacrifice. Analyzing Aztec human sacrifice, he noted that victims were brought into the circle of the sacrificers to enjoy the pleasures with them. Along this line, I take the pampering of the Roman gladiators before their fatal combat as another example. McAvan sees something similar happen in *The Hunger Games* when Katniss and Peeta are taken to the Capitol. They are drawn into the consumerist lifestyles of the Capitol, given fancy food—such as the lamb stew (lamb being a symbol for the sacrificed) that Katniss mentions during her interview with Caesar Flickerman—and beauty treatment, which gets Katniss out of her trousers and into a variety of dresses that caress her increasingly feminized body.

What is eventually sacrificed, or squandered, are the carefully produced luxurious commodities to which humans are reduced. While citizens of the Capitol chase rapidly changing fashion and keep gulping down and spitting out food, they also consume the luxurious tributes who fill up their television screen year after year. Here I emphasize that the annual Hunger Game is not just punishment, execution, or even sacrifice per se. It actually allows one child to survive and turns him or her into a celebrity. The game's goal is to perpetuate the competitive logic of the arena across Panem and promote a consumerist lifestyle among the citizens, despite the fact that the majority of them spend their entire lives struggling to make ends meet. In this sacrificial game, the spirit of neoliberal capitalism is sanctified.

The third line of theorization is Adorno and Horkheimer's discussion of ritual sacrifice as tied to the concept of mimesis and the development of scientific rationality. Following the lead of the Frankfurt school, Martin focuses on the connection between Panem's cruel games and the advanced technologies that undergird its sovereign power to make these games possible. It turns out that the sacralization of the political community and the economic order relies on science and technology, whose power over nature is again rooted in ritual sacrifice. In their *Dialectic of Enlightenment* (1993), Adorno and Horkheimer resorted to an anthropological understanding of mimesis developed by Walter Benjamin (1892–1940) in his essay "On the Mimetic Faculty." Benjamin saw mimesis as the gift of recognizing and producing similarities, something that ritual magic in ancient societies and technological reproduction in the modern world share in common. Instead of focusing on the sacrificed as either scapegoat or luxury, Adorno and Horkheimer explore the logic, or "ruse," of ritual sacrifice and how the shaman gains power in this process.

The tension that communities practicing ritual sacrifice face, according to Adorno and Horkheimer, is first and foremost located between humans and the extrahuman nature, not within the communities. In ritual sacrifice, the shaman endeavors to wield god-like power over nature. This power is obtained by exchanging an object of lesser value for something of greater value. The uniqueness of the object—the sacrificial victim—is at the heart of the shaman's attempt to influence events. However, the shaman also has to recognize and produce similarities between the victim and the desired greater good. This process of ritual substitution initiates the larger process of reducing nature to example and category and wiping off the uniqueness of the individual. Magic begins to progress toward science and technology, while myth is to be replaced by enlightenment. However, the story of progression is also one of regression, in that scientific rationality has become a new myth and a repressive one. To achieve domination over nature, humans now are dominated by their own power of abstraction—in other words, their instrumental reason.

Panem, a post-apocalyptic human community, practices ritual sacrifice, the Hunger Games, to wield "supernatural" powers—powers over a non-anthropocentric and undomesticated nature. The gamemakers are shaman-like figures who play gods within the arena by manipulating this artificial environment and freely altering its "natural" laws. The object of lesser value within the mini-world of the arena is the scapegoated tributes. The much-desired greater good is the docile bodies of all Panem citizens. The tributes, young children from the Districts, are unique, but they are also similar to the object of greater value, the ideal individual competing among themselves and submissive to the absolute power of Panem, which dominates both extrahuman nature and human society. It is no exaggeration to say that Panem, the ultimate gamemaker behind all gamemakers, aspires to become a deity-like entity that is omnipotent, omnipresent, and omniscient.

2.3 *Another Sacrifice Is Possible*

Sacrifice is a multifarious phenomenon that has produced a range of permutations of the sacred in the novels/films. The sacred community of Panem is haunted by the foundational violence of scapegoating; the sacred neoliberal order is a game of cut-throat competition and excessive expenditure; and the "supernatural" power of science and technology dominates the human and nonhuman in the name of freeing human culture from the domination of extrahuman nature. Under the all-seeing Eye of Panem, is another type of sacrifice possible? Has the logic of sacrifice surveyed in the previous section foreclosed any possibility of opening the sacred toward radical alterity?

The repressive sacrifice of the Hunger Games is counterpoised by the liberatory potential of the nonreciprocal, uncalculating, and self-abandoning sacrifice willingly embraced by the ordinary people. And, the sacred does not have to have a supernatural dimension or be monopolized by the dominant power. The sacred may very well irrupt between people—or bare life, if I may add some specification. Both McEvan and Williams turn to stories of willing self-sacrifice between friends and family. To give a few examples: Katniss offers herself to fight the hunger game as Prim's substitute; Rue, a tribute from District 11, dies protecting Katniss from a deadly attack; Thresh, another tribute from Rue's District, decides to keep Katniss alive at the expense of his own life because Katniss has helped Rue, his fellow tribute; Peeta and Katniss attempt to commit double suicide to deprive the game of a final winner (Collins 2008);

and in the Quarter Quell, Mags, a tribute from District 4, runs into poisonous gas so that Finnick, her partner, won't choose to save her instead of Peeta, a younger and stronger fighter for the revolution than herself (Collins 2009).

Whereas the "God" of Panem forces the tributes to sacrifice themselves for some greater good, some dare to undermine the logic of calculation, exchange, and the maximization of self-interest and to form collective bonds of solidarity even within the arena, a field of social Darwinism where winners and losers are pitted against each other. This is the counter-enchantment of the self-sacrificers, who do not seek empowerment at the expense of the other but abandon themselves for the good of the other. Analyzing these stories, Williams and McAvan bring up Levinas and Derrida. Reading Levinas's *Otherwise Than Being* (1998), Williams emphasizes Levinas's notion of the I as "hostage" to the other. Here the other is not the sovereign power of Panem but other powerless subjects. For Levinas, the self has an ethical obligation to the other and does not even think about receiving possible return from the other. No reciprocity exists between the self and the other. The meaning of love is dying for the other—the altruistic sacrifice of the self for the sake of the other.

Derrida made a similar point. McAvan focuses on his *Given Time* (1994) and *The Gift of Death* (1996). According to Derrida, true gift, like radical forgiveness, can never be good business. They are "aneconomic," beyond calculation. True forgiveness is impossible, consisting of forgiving the unforgivable. Likewise, true gift is giving to the other not to gain anything in return. Self-sacrifice is a true gift because while the other receives the given, what the I gains is her own death. Death, what is absolutely mine and entirely altruistic, cannot be exchanged. Hence, my death for the other, self-sacrifice, is the source of ethical responsibility to the other. McAvan views self-sacrifice in the trilogy as pointing "towards the fact that ethical relationships, even in neoliberalism, are not bound to calculation, that there remains an element that exceeds compelled competitive and violent relations ... a space whose alterity may or may not be God" (2017: 60).

Williams makes a distinction between imposed sacrifice linked to religious and political ends and willing self-sacrifice for loved ones and argues that "social change emerges only as a fragile byproduct" of the latter (2018: 76). What he contests is the claims of the god-like state that force children to die for the civic order. What he endeavors to restore is the self's obligation to the other as conceptualized by Levinas and Derrida. The sacred that McAvan contests is neoliberalism, a economic and socio-political order known for its commodification of everything. The alternative form of the sacred that she excavates from the series is "an unearned, unwarranted grace that points the way out of the ethical dead-end of neoliberal self-interest" (2017: 60) and "an intrusion of otherness, something else than sheer economy, unexpected, unwarranted, undeserved—and yet for all that, just and necessary" (2017: 61).

Endorsing Williams's insights, I see two shortcomings in his assertion. First, he polarizes secular, humanistic love and politics, with the latter labeled religious and repressive. There is also a deeply entrenched suspicion against the collective in his study. His warning against celebrating sacrifice, even the ethically responsible self-sacrifice, is a point well-taken. However, to reiterate McAvan's argument, when neoliberalism has been relentlessly undoing social bonds and human collectivities, to abandon the self for the benefits of the other is a crucial strategy of resistance. At this point, we may want to go back to the gladiator paradigm.

Reading Collins's novels as a contemporary retelling of the Spartacus story, Aitchison argues that the political lesson of both is that collective action must begin and end with familial love. In Aitchison's interpretation, although Collins is "skeptical as to the state's and the masses' capacity to put things right," her trilogy "takes up the same radical (if less doctrinaire) concern informing Fast's *Spartacus*; like Fast, Collins is bent on recuperating a family feeling that is antithetical to the self-interested individualism on which modern capitalism depends" (2015: 268). While Kathrine R. Broad critiques the epilogue of *The Hunger Games* series, which presents Katniss as a married woman with two kids (2013), Aitchison argues that family in the novels is not a heteronormative institution where the laboring individuals are reproduced but a site of brotherly and sisterly love, or self-sacrifice for the other, that promises genuine social change. Family may serve as a mediating ground for the individual and the collective, where we are prepared to resist the violence of Panem, the political, economic, and technological order of which is sacred.

Aitchison's reading resonates with Hubler's argument that Collins's trilogy is utopian. Hubler compares Lois Lowry's *The Givers* quartet (1993–2012) and Collins's trilogy. The former is anti-utopian, "manifest[ing] suspicion of utopian projects and project[ing] a static view of human nature as selfish and therefore incapable of creating and maintaining a just society without supernatural intervention" (2014: 241). By contrast, *The Hunger Games* trilogy is utopian. It presents the collective efforts of the ordinary people to create a better society by sacrificing themselves for people like themselves. They are able to disenchant the enchantment of the Hunger Games and institute their counter-enchantment. I find it problematic that Hubler locates the religious in the realm of the mythic, which stands in opposition to the realm of the historical (2014: 234–5). I agree with her that the tradition of dystopian fiction tends to avoid any positive figuration of collective experience, a tendency also observable in Williams's article. However, both Williams and Hubler misrepresent religion, the former blaming it for being political and repressive, the latter dismissing it as apolitical and escapist. While Williams pits humanistic love against repressive politics that is labeled religious, Hubler believes that the religious is removed from political realities and collective struggles.

I see *The Hunger Games* as a story that vividly illustrates the inseperability of religion and politics, or, more precisely, political economy backed up by science and technology. For the same reason I critique Williams and Hubler, I value McAvan's quest for the sacred in the self-other relationship between (non)human beings. The sacred is not set apart from the profane. Moreover, the sacred has two faces, one named Panem, the other the loving bond between the seemingly insignificant little selves who endeavor to create their own third space, their make-shift home, and the terrain of congruence. Bare life is not devoid of enchantment. Resistance against the sovereign power of Panem starts with singing, painting, and the making of an image called Mockingjay, topics of the next section.

3   Enchantment II: Bare Life and the Religion/Art of Resistance

Panem's state ritual is a machine of enchantment, but powerless individuals like Katniss also seek enchantment. They are not without a reservoir of tactics to cope with the unbearable burden that is life. They do religious/artistic work to reconfigure their sense of being-in-the-world, their relation to one another, and their perception of the world. This enchanting work is accomplished by Katniss's singing, Peeta's painting, and the human-nonhuman network evolving around the image of the mockingjay.

This section is divided into three parts. Part one is devoted to articles that take folk music as a spirituality that offers redemption to Katniss and many others. Parts two considers academic discussions centered upon Peeta's "useless" hobby, painting, as in contrast to the monstrous art of the Hunger Games. Part three follows existing scholarship to study the various iteration of the mockingjay, the very symbol of revolution, which is in turn a bird, a pin, a dress, and a girl. In these three parts, I put discussions on *The Hunger Games* novels/films in dialogue with some of the latest developments in the fields of religion and music, religion and visual art, and religion and material culture, respectively. It is to be emphasized that while sacrifice is *both* demanded by the sovereign power of Panem *and* willingly embraced by those who place the suffering of others above themselves, the enchantment of religion and art is thoroughly ambiguous as well. It is performed by the mega-machines of the authoritarian state and global capitalism to control the ordinary people, if not bare life per se, as analyzed in the previous section. It is also the tiny miracles created by Katniss and her loved ones in the midst of existential and political difficulties.

3.1   Katniss the Singer and the Spirituality of Music

Religion is not immediately visible in the fictional space of *The Hunger Games* novels/films. Likewise, Panem, where mass entertainment dominates, seems to be an artless land. However, we are to be reminded that religion is not limited to the post-Enlightenment model that foregrounds interiorized piety as separated from the messy realities of everyday life, or the putatively secular social spheres, just as art is not primarily defined by an exclusive concern with beauty and aesthetics. Studying religion and music in tandem, Heidi Epstein's *Melting the Venusberg: A Feminist Theology of Music* (2004) and Danielle Ann Lynch's *God in Sound and Silence: Music in Theology* (2018), among many other similar projects, question established tenets regarding the meaning and function of both religion and music. They have stepped outside the comfort zone of established religious traditions and the elite types of music to seek revelation in all areas of human life. For them, religion is not limited to established institutions, while music is both embodied experience and discursive practice embedded in social interactions and power struggles.

Moreover, Epstein's emphasis on a tragic sensibility and Lynch's reconceptualization of transcendence as liminality are worthy of our particular attention. According to Epstein, music is not just a power to resolve discords, maintain order and harmony, and offer spiritual transport to the privileged individual. On the contrary, music confronts violence and makes statements about tragedies in the world (2004). Similarly, for Lynch, transcendence does not mean freedom from one's physical embodiment and social political locatedness but liminality—the crossing of thresholds, the breaking of boundaries, and the call for and striving toward radical change (2018). I argue that this transcendence, informed by the tragic sensiblity Epstein highlights, is the very enchanting power of music unleashed by Katniss the singer.

Understanding Katniss as a singer of folk songs, Tammy L. Gant argues that music is a form of spirituality—that is, noninstitutionalized religion—that salvages the soul in the dystopian world (2014). In a similar light, Anne Torkelson (2014), Tina L. Hanlon (2012), Jon Fitzgerald and Philip Hayward (2015), Catherin Driscoll and Alexandra Heatwole (2018), and Kj Swanson (2016) have all discussed the enchantment of music in the novels/films.

Torkelson's article presents music as a power capable of shaping the moral character of individuals and collectives and bringing about social and political changes. Although Durkheim is not cited, what is implied is that music helps to build or break the sacred, either the sacred order of Panem or the sacred that irrupts in the struggles of the powerless. The theorist that Torkelson resorts to is Socrates (470–399 BCE), or, more precisely, Socrates as Plato's (428/427 or 424/423–348/347 BCE) mouthpiece in *The Republic*, who worried about the potential danger of music and urged his ideal society to outlaw certain types of music and musical instruments.

What Socrates meant by music is the Greek idea of mousikē, which encompasses the entire realm of the Muses, including music, visual art, and performative arts. In ancient Greece, mousikē, in contrast to gymnastics that cultivated the body, was endowed with the task to train the soul. In this training, music in a narrow sense played a crucial role because it imitated the emotions of life in its melodies, harmonies, and rhythms and was able to affect people, whose characters were shaped by different types of music, with good music cultivating good characters such as courageousness and caring, and bad music promoting vices such as a lack of self-control.

In Torkelson's consideration, Panem, a dystopian version of Plato's Republic, is acutely aware of the power of music. It bans songs such as "The Hanging Tree," a rally call for revolution (to be analyzed later). By contrast, although a singer and lover of folk songs, Katniss mistakes music for something frivolous, its value "somewhere between hair ribbons and rainbows" (Collins 2008: 211). As the story unfolds, she gradually learns to appreciate and wield the power of singing, one that challenges the enchantment of Panem by disenchanting its ideologies and re-enchanting human existence.

While Torkelson emphasizes the character-building or soul-shaping function of music, Gant claims that although "[t]here is no reference in the trilogy to a sacred set of beliefs or practices ... not even a reference to a higher power of any ilk beyond the oppressive government," Collins uses "the ubiquitous presence of folk songs, lullabies, and songbirds ... to fill the space meant for religion in Katniss's life" (2014: 89). For Gant, religion and art, both human-made systems, work "to develop and nurture the soul, ... the part of each of us that responds to beauty and morality and righteousness" (2014: 89). This resonates with Jackson, who contends that religion and art both originate from the human endeavor to change the world, or at least our perception of the world, and sees music as a form of spirituality that does religious work. And, the metaphysical dimension of music is not disconnected from its power to incite and promote social changes, as spiritual growth means finding one's place in the material world.

More specifically, Gant reads the singing of "The Meadow Song" as a ritual that Katniss performs for the dying Rue. In this ritual, Katniss comes to realize the moral failings of her culture and calls for repentance. When the mockingjays pick up the song and begin to sing, Katniss is depicted as feeling "eerie"

(Collins 2008: 235) and "unearthly" (Collins 2008: 329). It is "one of the few places in the text—each connected to music—where Collins uses language that connotates the transcendent" (Gant 2014: 91).

Another episode that Gant considers is Katniss's singing after her "dark night of the soul." Having lost Prim due to the weapon that Gale, a close friend of the sisters, has designed, Katniss assassinates President Coin instead of President Snow. She is imprisoned by the new government and refuses to speak. Several days later, after intense self-reflection, she decides to embrace life and bursts out singing "[h]our after hour of ballads, love songs, mountain airs" (Collins 2010: 375). This act of singing is another enchanting ritual in which she regains some control over a broken life.

Finally, in the epilogue of the last novel, the lyrics of "The Meadow Song" are repeated when Katniss watches her children play, indicating that she is able to overcome the existential difficulties that keep her and other humans from fulfillment and flourishing. Gant concludes by claiming that "[i]n music she finds the courage to face the Capitol's atrocities, the strength to forge her own path, and the healing to survive the trauma that has been her life story. In the finale of the score of her life, music takes center stage in restoring her soul" (2014: 96).

Resonating with Gant, Hanlon points out that what helps to rescue Katniss's humanity is folk music in particular—"the ballads and mountain airs she … learned from her father and recalls during some of her most painful crises" (2012: 65). Hanlon also notices that the dance Katniss and Prim perform at a war-time wedding "could be referring to Appalachian clogging or flatfoot dancing" (2012: 65). The fictional District 12 where the protagonists are from is modeled after the real Appalachia. I add that the folk songs that Katniss sings are shared by many people—her family, her District, and other Districts, all of which form a collective that does not overlap with the nation of Panem as controlled by the Capitol. Moreover, this alternative collective cuts across the boundaries between the fictional realm and our real-life world (as to be demonstrated in section 5, which deals with transmedia storytelling or world-building).

The connection between the fictional "mountain airs" in the 2012 film *The Hunger Games* and Appalachian folk music in our world is the research topic of Fitzgerald and Hayward's article. While Collins merely describes folk songs in her novels, the Lionsgate film is able to translate words into audio-visual texts. Fitzgerald and Hayward demonstrate how the filmic sounds draw from the repository of Appalachian music, commenting that "the pre-modern Anglo-Celtic tradition, and the 'cultural capital' of the economically impoverished Appalachian community that retains it, lends symbolic weight and context to the role of song in the novel and film, evoking a cultural continuity and dignity for the inhabitants of District 12, and Katniss Everdeen in particular, that stands in stark contrast to the shallow and superficial world of the Capitol, with its garish fashions and modern media fixations" (2015: 77).

Fitzgerald and Hayward then bring it to the reader's attention that Appalachia boasts of Anglo-Celtic songs (not really "folk") and a less celebrated variety of other musical materials, such as African American songs and instrumental materials. However, Collins's novel and the film based on it perpetuate this imbalance. Moreover, with the extension of the novel into the film, ancillary audio-visual texts are conceived. In this regard, Fitzgerald and Hayward study the difference between "The Meadow Song" as described in the novel and how it appears in the film. While the novel first mentions the song when Rue, at the end of her life, asks for a song from Katniss in the arena, the film actually begins with Katniss and Prim together singing the song in their home. This lullaby inspires the song and promotional video "Safe and Sound" by Taylor Swift and the musical duo The Civil Wars. The end-credits of the film are accompanied by three original song texts: "Safe and Sound," Arcade Fire's "Abraham's Daughter," and The Civil Wars' "Kingdom Come." All three feature prominently on a CD album entitled *The Hunger Games: Songs from District 12 and Beyond*. The folk music from Appalachia, through the mediation of *The Hunger Games* novel/film, merges into a highly-profitable commodity.

The claim I make on the basis of Fitzgerald and Hayward's work is that the counter-enchantment of Katniss's singing, one that resists the sovereign power of Panem, is folded back into the enchantment of creative industry and cultural consumption in our world. However, I do not deny the possibility of consumers exercising their agency to challenge media corporations and pursue alternative enchantment. Morgan has made an excellent point that enchantment, disenchantment, and re-enchantment is an always ongoing process. Driscoll and Heatwole remind the reader that although the folk songs "are emblems of a life outside the rule of the Capitol, heightened by taking a pre-industrial form like song in an age of digital media technology ...[they] only reach the pitch of communicability and popularity anchoring revolution via industrialized mass production, resembling the Nazi use of folk culture in Weimar Germany as much as the popularity of recovered and new ballad forms in 1960s alternative culture" (2018: 78). They are acutely aware of the indeterminacy of enchantment. Back in the fictional space, Katniss's singing is indeed recorded by the rebels from District 13 and used as war propaganda. Most ironically, District 13 turns out to be another Panem, which Katniss has to rebel against. There is no end in sight to the fight over enchantment.

The last piece I survey is Swanson's article, which studies the soundtracks of the first two films: *The Hunger Games* and *Catching Fire*. Swanson's task, not unlike that of Gant, is to look for religion in the religion-less novels/films. Unlike Gant, who presents music as an elementary form of religious/artistic experience, Swanson looks beyond the original novels/films to study the religious, or, more specifically, Christian, vocabulary and motifs of the pop songs collected in the two albums. The first was produced by T. Bone Burnett. The producer of the second is Alexandra Patsavas. Swanson demonstrates that the songs that are meant to illustrate Collins's "secular" story-world actually contain 1) symbolic terms that include angel, saint, demon, and martyr; 2) specific religious terminology such as heaven, devil, prayer, God, and even biblical names and references including "Christ-like"; and 3) contextual references to religion such as baptism, sacrifice, and eschatology (Swanson 2016: 28–30).

Among the songs, "Abraham's Daughter" covers all three categories described above. This song reinterprets the story of Abraham's binding of Isaac from Genesis 22 and inserts a Katniss-like daughter figure who uses her bow and arrow to demand the release of Isaac (Swanson 2016: 30). The Judeo-Christian[6] tradition that Panem's North American predecessor (that is, our world) is familiar with, although not alluded to in the original novels, manifests itself when the novels extend into other media formats, such as the films and the songs. The use of religious imagery can be explained by considering "the borrowed terminology of rural religious tradition expressed through conventional assumptions of Appalachian music, the soteriological and eschatological concerns conveyed in the apocalyptic functions of contemporary dystopia, ... [and] the secularization of sacred terms as disseminated through postmodern popular culture" (Swanson 2016: 36). In short, religion has never been absent, although the types of enchantment it performs has taken on new shapes.

It is interesting to note that not only scholars but also fans have discussed Katniss's songs. As early as August 25–26, 2010, a fan named John Granger posted two articles discussing "The Hanging Tree" and "The Meadow Song" at his personal website www.hogwartsprofessor.com. He pointed out the possible connection between "The Hanging Tree" and "Strange Fruit," an anti-racist ballad most famously recorded by Billie Holliday, reading the tree as the Cross and the hanged man a Christ-figure (2010a). He then argued that the image of the meadow in "The Meadow Song" is the theme of redemption of the entire series

---

6 It is to be pointed out that Swanson used the term "Judeo-Christian" without paying attention to its diverse usages and complex history, not to mention the differences between the two traditions. For a survey of how the term was used in the American context, see Silk 1984; Britt 2012.

(2010b). In 2014, after the release of the third movie, "Mockingjay—Part 1," at least two more online articles highlighted the origin of "The Hanging Tree" in "Strange Fruit" and the former's indebtedness to civil rights protest songs (Weber 2014; Mason 2014). Inspired by this line of thinking, I take another look at these songs.

In Collins's trilogy, Katniss altogether sings three songs. The first two—"The Meadow Song" and "The Hanging Tree"—have been extensively discussed.[7] However, the ignored third song still needs to be explored. I call it "The Valley Song," the lyrics of which are never given. In the first novel, it is merely mentioned by Peeta when he helps Katniss inside the game arena and confesses his feelings for her. In Peeta's memory, Katniss sang it on the first day of school in music assembly and made "every bird outside the windows [fall] silent" (Collins 2008: 301). "The Meadow Song" is often named "Rue's Lullaby" or "The Valley Song" by critics and fans. However, I argue that "The Valley Song" is not to be confused with "The Meadow Song," because the former serves as a tie between Katniss and Peeta, while the latter is the song shared by Katniss and two other girls, Prim and Rue.

In the Appalachian area, "Down in the Valley" is a country blues song popular in the 1920s. It may have inspired both "The Valley Song" and "The Meadow Song," with the former borrowing its central image of the valley, while the lyrics of the latter imitates those of the real-world song. For instance, the first two lines of "Down in the Valley" read as "Down in the valley, the valley so low/Hang your head over, hear the wind blow," while "The Meadow Song" begins with "Deep in the meadow, under the willow/A bed of grass, a soft green pillow."

There are many versions of "Down in the Valley," performed and recorded by various artists and with varying lyrics. What's worth noticing is that the song is also titled "Birmingham Jail." Guitarist Jimmie Tarlton claimed to have written the lyrics in 1925 while he was in Birmingham Jail for moonshining. So, the first-person "I" that yearns for his lover is incarcerated. And, this "I" is not some individual but represents an entire community. He is addressing his lover from the Birmingham City Jail, the same place that Martin Luther King Jr. wrote his open letter against racism in 1963. The lyrics of "Down in the Valley," against this background, make a public statement that is to be performed again and again and remembered across generations.

---

7 For discussion of "The Meadow Song," see Torkelson 31–33; Gant 91–93, 97; Hanlon 65; Fitzgerald and Hayward; Driscoll and Heatwole 77; for "The Hanging Tree," see Torkelson 33–36; Gant 96; Hanlon 66; Driscoll and Heatwole 77.

In light of the history of the original "Down in the Valley," the romantic relationship between Peeta and Katniss mediated by a song is not without its political undertone—their solidarity based on a shared yearning for freedom and justice. Peeta is not just a gentle boy in love with Katniss but also the very one who boldly claims that he does not want to be owned by those wielding power over life and death.

The other song, "The Meadow Song," links Katniss to two girls: Prim, her younger sister, and Rue, the little girl from District 11, who, in the arena, offers help to her competitor Katniss and forms an alliance with her. "The Meadow Song" is a song of care, urging the living to take care of the young, the weak, and the fallen. It is a soothing lullaby Katniss sings to put Prim to sleep as well as the funeral song devoted to Rue after she is killed protecting Katniss. While decorating the latter's body with wild flowers, Katniss sings to her this song, whose value is "somewhere between hair ribbons and rainbows." It is this "useless" song, performed as part of the burial ritual and broadcast to the audiences of the Hunger Games, that triggers the rebellion that eventually ends the rule of the Capitol.

Then there is "The Hanging Tree," which is strictly banned in Panem. As a little girl, Katniss learned "The Hanging Tree" from her father, who died of a mining accident. She was scolded by her mother when she sang it, because the song was dangerous and forbidden. The lyrics are dark and disturbing, with the lyric "I" being a dead man calling out for his love to join him and flee the world. In the last novel, Katniss, having joined the rebellion against the Capitol, travels with a camera crew to shoot a propaganda film. Upon the request of Pollux, a tongue-less cameraman, she sings the heart-wrenching "The Hanging Tree." Her impromptu performance is filmed and edited. In the novel, the footage is never aired. However, the song does become war propaganda in the last two films.

Again, the fictional "Hanging Tree" pays tribute to a pre-existing song, "Strange Fruit," the famous anti-lynching song written by the Jewish poet and songwriter Abel Meeropol (1903–1986) and performed by singers such as Billie Holiday (1915–1959). She is the subject matter of Tracy Fessenden's book *Religion Around Billie Holiday*, which provides a detailed history of the song (2018: 156–160). Considering this lyric intertextuality, the hanging tree is the lynching tree from which strange fruits (that is, dead bodies) are hanging. What's more, in the lyrics of "The Hanging Tree," the word *strange* is repeated several times: "Strange things did happen here/No stranger would it be."

Here we are to be reminded that "The Hanging Tree" was influenced by both "Strange Fruit" and "Down in the Valley." Resembling the latter, "The Hanging

Tree" is a call from the lyric "I" addressed at "you," which is his/her lover, anyone from the Districts, or the reader outside the fictional space. Wearing "a necklace of rope/hope" (the word "rope" in the original changed into "hope" in the filmic song), the lyric "I" calls out to "you" to flee. Who is the dead man having "murdered three"? Where would he and his lover escape to?

James Cone, always interested in the theological implications of the spirituals and the blues (1980), specifically brings up Holiday's "Strange Fruit" in his book *The Cross and the Lynching Tree* (2011). Cone forcefully argues that in America, in addition to the cross, the undeniable central image of Christianity, there is another cross that major Christian theologians have overlooked while the African Americans have to bear it: the lynching tree. The lynching tree, or the hanging tree, is also a Christian symbol. It is captured in songs that attest to the suffering of the black people who strive for liberation from oppression and slavery. The film adaptations of Collins's novels "whitewashed" some characters—including Katniss, who may be colored—and chose not to explore the fictional songs' indebtedness to the struggle against racism of which black liberation theology is an integral part. However, "The Hanging Tree" remains a sacramental song. The dead man is a revolutionary, or a Christ-like figure of radical politics, although not necessarily the Christian God. While the imprisoned man in "Down in the Valley" yearns to transcend his confinement and dreams about radical freedom, the dead man calls out from beyond to the suffering masses to critique and challenge the established powers of this world and strive for true liberation from the status quo. The imprisoned and the dead are the same lyric "I" that works to build a new community for the oppressed.

3.2 *The Mimetic Art of Peeta the Painter*

A parallel to Katniss's singing is Peeta's painting. Peeta, another protagonist of the novel, has also been extensively studied. Although much attention has been paid to his loving, nurturing masculinity, an unconventional gender role (Lem and Hassel 2012; Taber et al. 2013), his hobby of painting has been downplayed in the film adaptations and largely overlooked in relevant expositions. While current scholarship on religion and visual art[8] has been focused on the

---

8 Diane Apostolos-Cappadona's *Religion and the Arts: History and Method* (2017) is an excellent introduction to anyone interested in the field of religion and the arts. It surveys the history and method of this field from the nineteenth century to the present. In addition, *The Oxford Handbook of Religion and the Arts* (2014) edited by Frank Burch Brown consists of a collection of essays that showcases the diverse religious traditions and art forms covered in this field.

artist and/or the artistic object rather than the work of religion/art as theorized by Jackson, discussion of Peeta's work of religion/art helps to shed light on a new direction for this particular field of inquiry. What is to be emphasized is that neither religion nor art is separable from society and politics, and that both are diffused in everyday struggles.

Among scholars who read *The Hunger Games* series, Brian McDonald is the only one who sees an artist in Peeta. McDonald's 2012 article invokes Aristotle's (385–322 BCE) notion of art as mimesis to argue that Peeta is an artist-hero whose mimetic art confronts the monstrous art of Panem. In his 2014 article, McDonald further develops his argument, presenting Peeta the artist-hero as a Socrates figure who helps Katniss learn how to live a life of critical reflection. Like Katniss the singer, Peeta the painter also performs counter-enchantment to create a third space, an existential home, and a fleeting moment of congruence in a world of incongruency.

In his 2012 article, McDonald presents Peeta as an artist who attends to and cares for the things represented. The mimesis practiced by Peeta is "imagination's attempt to represent something in a fictional form that exists in the real world" and "the highest testimony to the fact that human beings are the most imitative of living creatures" (2012: 10). Moreover, artistic mimesis has an elevating and redemptive power. To substantiate his claim, McDonald calls our attention to two episodes. In the first novel, when the tributes receive training at the camouflage station, Peeta weaves artful designs from objects available at hand. Katniss notices on his arm "the alternating patterns of light and dark [that] suggest sunlight falling through leaves in the woods" and wonders how he is able to create them without her own hunting and gathering experience, thinking he most likely does so just by looking at "the scraggly old apple tree in his backyard" (Collins 2008: 95). Later in the arena, Peeta relies on his camouflage art to save both himself and Katniss. In this case, what is illustrated is Jackson's thesis that art as a pragmatic technique is able to alter our state of existence and change our perception of the world. What Peeta accomplishes is the use of camouflage to make himself and Katniss invisible in the eyes of the other tributes. Art literally saves their lives.

The second episode McDonald interprets is from the second novel. When Peeta and Katniss are forced into the arena to fight the Quarter Quell, their new opponents include two morphlings, survivors of some previous games. Like Peeta, they are painters good at the art of camouflage. The female morphling saves Peeta from the attack of mutant monkeys and is fatally injured herself (another example of self-sacrifice). Before she dies, Peeta comforts her by describing his painting experience:

> With my paint box at home, I can make every color imaginable. Pink. As pale as a baby's skin. Or as deep as rhubarb. Green like spring grass. Blue that shimmers like ice on water.... One time, I spent three days mixing paint until I found the right shade for sunlight on white fur. You see, I kept thinking it was yellow, but it was much more than that. Layers of all sorts of color. One by one.
> COLLINS 2009: 312

In Peeta's experience of mixing paint, McDonald discerns the delight of learning and a form of communion with beauty. This experience is the best thing Peeta can share with the dying morphling, who is an artist too:

> Beneath her bodily agony, beneath the layers of drug addiction and despair, at the deepest strata of her being is one who loves beauty and longs to reproduce it through artistic mimesis.
> MCDONALD 2012: 12

At the last moment of her life, she even tries to reciprocate by drawing with her fingers the outline of a flower on Peeta's cheek.

What stands in stark contrast to Peeta's mimesis is the monstrous art of the Capitol, one that intends to disfigure nature. Examples of this monstrous art range from the seemingly innocuous bodily modifications to the heinous fight-to-the-death Hunger Games. McDonald sees the Hunger Games in particular as an exaggeration of our reality in which "entertainment became the whole point of life, and the appetite for excitement swept away all of the limits formerly enforced by our battered moral sensibilities" (2012: 9). In his eyes, the horrible ethic of the arena is matched by the freakish aesthetic of the Remake Center and the grotesque fashion of the Capitol, the latter two comparable to the drive towards de-creation—the perversities of destruction—in much of modern and postmodern art and literature.

McDonald's hostility toward reality TV (the topic of the next section) and postmodern art (represented by Andres Serrano's *The Piss Christ*) is misplaced. Moreover, I disagree with his argument that the sacred is absent in Panem, where what binds a society together is not a sense of shared obligations but sheer coercive power. I argued in the previous section that the political, economic, and technoscientific order of Panem, although dystopian, is sacred, while its repressive enchantment is irreducible to sheer coercive power. However, I give credit to McDonald's point that Panem is evil because it attempts to play God (2014). The thrill at desecration and destruction comes from a perverse imitation of God, who creates the moral law and is above its constraints. By breaking the law gratuitously, humans gain an illusion that they are free from the restraints of the moral law as is God. By imitating God to (de)create one's own and others' bodies, people of the Capitol, especially its rulers, seek omnipotence, or at least the psychological illusion of omnipotence.

It is Augustine's (354–430 AD) reflection on evil in *Confessions* that McDonald brings up in both articles. The 2014 piece argues that systemic evil must be overcome rather than simply fought against. Reflections on the nature, motives, and mechanisms of moral evil are necessary. In addition to Augustine's discussion of perverse will, he introduces Socrates and Hannah Arendt (1906–1975), who explain evil as ignorance and banality, respectively. Confronting the three faces of evil—ignorance, banality, and the perverse will to imitate God—we need to practice a life of critical examination, independent judgment, and careful and caring mimesis that enhances life instead of destroying it. The 2012 article makes clear the idea that while Katniss is the hero, Peeta is the redeemer. This article emphasizes that Peeta the artist-hero is a Socratic figure who plays a midwifery role in relation to Katniss, who, in her struggle against the evil of Panem, must learn to abandon an unexamined life, to think independently rather than seek social conformity, and to show love and respect to what is given in the world.

To illustrate the point mentioned above, McDonald zooms in on the episode in which Peeta talks to Katniss on a rooftop in the arena (2014). Peeta says: "I keep wishing I could think of a way to … to show the Capitol they don't own me. That I'm more than just a piece in their Games" (Collins 2008: 142). Although Katniss does not understand what he means, later, when the dying Rue begs her to sing, she suddenly recalls Peeta's words, realizing that

> I want to do something, right here, right now, to shame them, to show the Capitol that whatever they do or force us to do there is part of every tribute they can't own. That Rue was more than a piece in their Games. And so am I.
> COLLINS 2008: 236–237

The singer in Katniss who dedicates her song to Rue in front of the reality TV cameras to ignite a revolution against the Capitol is brought into the world by Peeta. McDonald also points out that there is a parallel in Katniss burying Rue and what Peeta does for the morphling:

> In their partnership, Peeta seems to be Katniss's mentor in discovering Truth just as he seems to serve as a powerful example of Goodness, but

they both discover and embody the given Beauty in the world through parallel but independent routes. Katniss invokes beauty through her songs and Peeta through art.

2014: 80

Thanks to their religious/artistic work, enchantment is not monopolized by the deity-like Panem.

3.3 *Mockingjay, the Image at Work*

Both the repressive enchantment of Panem, exemplified by the state ritual of the Hunger Games, and the liberatory enchantment of Katniss the singer and Peeta the painter are activated by images. According to Morgan, what plays a key role in human interaction with nonhuman things is images, which "operate as the tokens of enchantment by deftly integrating the individual into larger communities or networks of human and nonhuman actants, which is where the extended work of enchantment takes place" (2018: 18). What images achieve is metamorphosis, the change of something into something else in our perception, because they are able to bring into being an alternative world by bending the rules of conventional appearances. The image of the mockingjay is a perfect example in this case. This image is multifarious, the shifting iterations of which form a network of human and nonhuman objects.

Within the story-world of the novels/films, the mockingjay is the symbol of the resistance force against Panem, or, more precisely, the Capitol. Upon closer scrutiny, the mockingjay turns out to be many things: a bird, a pin, a dress, and a girl named Katniss. First of all, the mockingjay is the hybrid offspring of the jabberjay and the mockingbird. The jabberjay is a genetically engineered bird created by the Capitol to spy on the people of the Districts. However, after the rebels learn to feed it with false information, the jabberjay project is abandoned. Left in the wild, the all-male jabberjays mate with the mockingbirds to produce a new breed, the mockingjay, a songbird that can imitate human voices and sing human songs (Collins 2008: 50; 2009: 91–92). Participating in Katniss's singing, the mockingjay has been duly analyzed by scholars who study music in the novels/films (Gant 2012; Fitzgerald and Hayward 2015).

The mockingjay is also a pin that the mayor's daughter Madge gives to Katniss before the game, showing a bird flying in a circle of gold. Katniss cherishes the mockingjay pin because her father used to sing with these birds. She says that having it is "like having a piece of my father with me, protecting me" (Collins 2008: 50). In the arena, she makes friends with Rue thanks to the pin, because Rue also loves the mockingjays' songs, notices the image on the pin, and decides to trust her (Collins 2008: 211–212). In the second novel, before the

Quarter Quell, it is the pin that Cinna, Katniss's stylist and an undercover rebel, uses to mark the tracker implanted in her arm so that it can be removed by the rebels when they save her from the arena (Collins 2009: 57).

The third iteration of the mockingjay is the wedding dress that Cinna designs for Katniss. She wears it to the interview right before the Quarter Quell. "Heavy white silk with a low neckline and tight waist and sleeves that fall from my wrists to the floor" (Collins 2009: 247), the dress burns when she spins in front of the audience and metamorphoses into another dress "the color of coal and made of tiny feathers" (Collins 2009: 252). In this way, the white gown transforms into a mockingjay. Or, the mockingjay dress transforms Katniss into a mockingjay and demonstrates to the audience that revolution is very much alive. In section 4, I will introduce the scholarly discussion of the mockingjay dress (van Dyke 2012; Byrne 2015; Montz 2012, 2016).

Finally, Katniss, the girl on fire, is a mockingjay among many others. Reading the jabberjay as the Capitol's failed strategy to dominate its people, Sean Connors presents the hybrid mockingjay as a tactic of the powerless and conflates it with the figure of Katniss, who is manipulated by the Capitol and then District 13 but, in and through resorting to a series of tactics, eventually finds her own voice in the wild (2014a). Similarly, Jill Olthouse takes Katniss as the mockingjay in deciphering the conversation between Katniss and Rue when they meet in the arena. Rue tells Katniss that people in her District use the mockingjays to send messages, and that these birds are nasty if you come near their nests. In Olthouse's reading, Katniss is a mockingjay fighting to protect her nest, which expands from her family to all the repressed people (2012).

Among scholars who view Katniss as the mockingjay, Lykke Guanio-Uluru has produced a particularly interesting piece (2017). She focuses on three strands that link Katniss and the mockingjay: birdsong, the feathered dress, and the convergence of the natural and the artificial. The first two have already been discussed by other scholars, while the last one is an argument against the interpretations offered by Conner (2014b) and Fitzgerald and Hayward (2015). The latter three see the mockingjay as symbolizing the final triumph of nature over the human attempts at de-creation through the means of technology. By contrast, Guanio-Uluru questions the rigid divide between the natural and the unnatural, the human and the nonhuman. I assume she would also critique McDonald's condemnation of the Capitol's monstrous art and his praise of Peeta's loving imitation of nature. For her, the ideal work of religion/art, the counter-enchantment against Panem's sovereign power, is not uncorrupted nature but the merging of Katniss and the mockingjay and the blurring of the boundaries between a technologically constructed and a naturally given self.

While the Capitol abandons the jabberjays, they survive in the wild. Likewise, Guanio-Uluru highlights that at the end of the novels/films, the body of Katniss is no longer a natural one, having been disciplined by the fashion system of Panem and modified by the Capitol and the Rebels. After the bombing that kills Prim, she is severely burned and receives skin transplants, her body "like a bizarre patchwork quilt" (Collins 2010: 397), consisting of both laboratory-grown cells and patches of her former self. This patchwork is not only the posthuman self of Katniss but also the human-nonhuman framework in which enchantment is at play, according to Morgan. Katniss is the focal object of the mockingjay, which is an assemblage of human and nonhuman actants.

Guanio-Uluru argues that Katniss gradually develops a posthuman identity by identifying with the half natural, half artificial figure of the mockingjay. Or, to bring together Jackson and Morgan, the self-empowering enchantment of Katniss is also self-abolishing in that she learns to submit to the agency of the nonhuman other and embrace a new posthuman subject. Guanio-Uluru acknowledges that the term posthuman refers to "a range of possible radical changes faced by contemporary humanity in response to recent technological advances that challenge and destabilize the boundaries between human, animal, and machine" (2017: 57). Staying away from positions such as technoscientific transhumanism that aspire to abandon embodiment, she sides with Donna Haraway, a philosophical-cultural posthumanist who calls for a radical reconfiguration of the human subject to accommodate the human others, other life forms, and artificial machines.

In the end, it is worth mentioning that Guanio-Uluru studies not just the mockingjay within the text but also the image of the mockingjay that graces the original book covers of *The Hunger Games* trilogy and the posters for the film adaptations. The mockingjay is the very image that mediates between the fictional realm and our real-life world. Designed by artist Tim O'Brien in collaboration with his wife, Elizabeth Parisi, the creative director for hardcover books at Scholastic, the image of the mockingjay gradually transforms from book one through two to three, showing the process by which the bird breaks out and soars free. The same image is then used in the film posters and appears within the films as the very symbol for revolution. Guanio-Uluru also studies the UK covers of *The Hunger Games* book series, which show a crucified bird resembling the phoenix, aligning "the books with the high-grossing *Harry Potter* series and its emphasis on both Christian symbolism and the symbol of the phoenix" (2017: 62).

However, to cite Morgan repeatedly, enchantment, or the work of religion/art, is intrinsically ambiguous. The message conveyed by the symbol of the mockingjay is indeterminate. If we look beyond the narrowly defined textual boundaries, this image is thoroughly ambiguous in the age of media convergence and transmedia storytelling (see section 5 for further discussion). After all, Katniss's songs have been coopted into the machine of capitalist capture and have lost their revolutionary edge. Maybe the very fact that Peeta's hobby of painting is left out by the films altogether is good news. The redemptive potential of mimetic art still awaits the reader's investigation and retrieval. The intertwining of the repressive and liberatory enchantments within and beyond the story-world of *The Hunger Games* novels/films is a theme the next three sections will wrestle with.

4   The Split Enchantment of *The Hunger Games* Reality Show

The previous two sections worked in tandem to demonstrate that enchantment, the work of religion/art, is a double-edged sword. It exacerbates repression in the hands of Panem and kindles hope for freedom and justice in the hearts of the repressed. To examine the entanglement of these two types of enchantment, I look beyond the Hunger Games fought within the arenas to consider *The Hunger Games* reality show. While the sovereign power of premodern regimes orders public torture and executions to terrorize the audience, Panem's television network turns the entire nation into a huge audience for this state-sanctioned ritual sacrifice, which terrorizes the Districts and entertains the Capitol. Broadcast as a reality program, the Hunger Games become *The Hunger Games* show, a media spectacle and a mechanism of enchantment. Studying the show, I address four questions in this section: 1) What is reality TV? 2) How is *The Hunger Games* show, an enchanting machine controlled by Panem, analyzed in existing scholarship? 3) According to existing scholarship, what is the counter-enchantment irrupting in the space of reality TV, which is not a closed text? 4) How must the relationship between religion and media in the age of reality TV be rethought?

4.1   *Reality TV: The Entertaining Real*
In an interview with Hannah Trierweiler Hudson, Collins explained that the idea of enacting a reality TV program as the center of her story came to her when she was channel-hopping between the news footage of young soldiers fighting and dying in the Iraqi war and scenes of a reality TV show. Arguing that our potential for desensitization—that is, seeking a voyeuristic thrill in watching other people suffer—was the real tragedy, Collins advocated a conscientious viewership that refuses to reduce lives of other people into raw material

for entertainment (Hudson 2010). Although the brutality of *The Hunger Games* show is her fictional invention, this fiction is based on our everyday life, of which reality TV is an integral part. What is reality TV? Why did Collins adopt this genre for the broadcast of the Hunger Games?

Reality TV is currently a major force within television culture. Although the interactive format can be traced to earlier traditions of radio and television, reality programs began to proliferate in the last two decades of the twentieth century and further developed stylistically and generically in the early years of the new millennium. Susan Murray and Laurie Ouellette define reality TV as "an unabashedly commercial genre united less by aesthetic rules or certainties than by the fusion of popular entertainment with a self-conscious claim to the discourse of the real" (2009: 3). They identify the selling point of reality programming as a playful look into the "entertaining real," which promises to provide "nonscripted" access to the "real" life of "ordinary" people with profit-making the end goal. For them, reality TV distances itself from fictional programs on the one hand, using minimal writing and nonprofessional actors to fixate on "authentic" people, situations, and stories rather than fictional content. On the other hand, reality programs, bypassing questions such as the responsibilities associated with truth claims and the ethical concerns over representing human subjects, are distinct from information formats such as news and documentaries.

In short, reality TV provides viewers with an allegedly unmediated look into the cultivated dramatic uncertainties of everyday life to satisfy their voyeuristic desires and lure them in as active participants who vote, chat, create user-generated content online, and make donations that impact the fates of those participants inside the shows. The surge of reality TV is embedded in the larger context of neoliberalization, which is the promotion of privatization, consumer choice, and personal responsibility (Ouellette and Hay 2008). In the neoliberal present, global capitalism has instituted a permanent state of emergency. To fight against outer and inner social threats, governments, corporations, and individuals have installed surveillance cameras everywhere, turning the world into a camera-saturated reality TV studio. Moreover, the state has retreated from providing social welfare, entrusting the management of social needs and risks to private sectors such as the TV industry. What follows is that the social function of reality TV is to accustom us to the surveillance society (Ouellette and Murray 2009) and to train the self-enterprising good citizens as the desired political subjects (Bourdon 2008; Ouellette and Hay 2008).

Reality TV is one particular component in an entire network of technologies designed to exercise disciplinary power to train the neoliberal individual, "whose most pressing obligation to society is to empower her or himself privately" (Ouellette and Hay 2008: 3). As introduced in section 1, Foucault borrowed the image of the panopticon from Bentham and contended that panoptic, disciplinary societies began to rise in the early nineteenth century. Now disciplinary society has evolved into what David Lyon calls surveillance societies "dependent on communication and information technologies for administrative and control processes" (2001: 1). We are subject to the omnipresent gaze of cameras and—in leaving digital footprints online—make ourselves visible and accessible to governments and corporations.

In addition to the rise of disciplinary power, Foucault discussed the transformation of pastoral power (Foucault 1999; Carrette 1999). Originating in Christian institutions, pastoral power has taken on a new political shape and been integrated into the modern Western state, or, more specifically, the welfare state. While the pastoral power of the Christian church was oriented at other-worldly salvation, its modern mutation has its object in assisting people to pursue worldly concerns such as health, wealth, and security. The welfare state conjoins the centralized power of the state and the individualization of pastorship "to ensure, sustain and improve the lives of each and every one" (Foucault 1999: 141). Supplementing disciplinary power, pastoral power also works to constitute the subject. Instead of imposing the gaze upon the individuals, pastoral power seeks to extract information from them through confessional strategies. In Foucault's words, "this form of power cannot be exercised without knowing the inside of people's minds, without exploring their souls, without making them reveal their innermost secrets. It implies a knowledge of the conscience and an ability to direct it" (1982: 783).

Reality TV is an instrument of disciplinary power. In this regard, Mark Andrejevic has critiqued reality TV for achieving interactivity at the expense of the participants, who are subject to constant surveillance (2004), or, in Collins's language, the voyeuristic gaze of an unsympathetic audience. Ouellette and Murray point out that the agenda of reality programs is to accustom both participants and audiences, who constantly interact with each other, to surveillance inside and outside the studios. These programs help to mitigate our resistance to the omnipresence of surveillance. In a variety of programs, "ordinary" people, both the performers and the viewers as potential participants, are encouraged to expose themselves to surveillance cameras and/or participate in watching and recording others and themselves. To be good citizens in the new millennium, "we must allow ourselves to be watched as we watch ourselves and those around us, and then modify our conduct and behavior accordingly" (Ouellette and Murray 2009: 9).

A microcosmic encapsulation of our surveillance society, reality TV also takes over the pastoral power of the welfare state and educational institutions.

Having learned to enjoy the presence of the cameras, we should be willing to perform in front of them. Jérôme Bourdon notices that the participants of reality TV shows must manage their images by exhibiting their physical and moral selves as well as the relational capacities required by the ever-escalating service economy. In other words, these disciplined docile bodies must manage themselves as projects located in social networks to adapt to an unstable and uncertain market (Bourdon 2008). In this market, another major responsibility of reality TV is to circulate practical guidelines for better living.

While commercialization has been extending into all aspects of life, including domestic work, personal appearance, and intimate relationships, television, which converges with other media, has been wielding its power "to access and guide the ethics, behaviors, aspirations, and routines of ordinary people" (Ouellette and Hay 2008: 2). These people expose themselves and their problems to the public in order to learn how to reflect on, manage, and improve their lives and "empower" themselves by watching and participating in reality TV shows. "As the state entrusts private entities (including TV) to operate as social service providers, conflict mediators, and support networks, popular reality TV does more than entertain—it becomes a resource for inventing, managing, caring for, and protecting ourselves as citizens" (Ouellette and Hay 2008: 4).

Reality TV shows that feature lifestyles make available an entire range of techniques geared to helping "needy" individuals transform into self-enterprising and self-actualizing neoliberal citizens. These techniques are packaged as guidelines from experts who are not cold personalities lecturing from a distance but self-trained ordinary people seemingly no different from the audience. There are some reality shows that literally function as social welfare programs, providing housing and healthcare to the lucky few among the participants. The pastoral power of these charity-themed and lifestyle shows, which offer expert guidance on everyday activities ranging from food and fashion to interpersonal relationships, endeavors to reach inside the social subjects. Reality TV is never short of moments of confession and emotional turmoil, which render those shows more dramatic, entertaining, and pastoral.

Scholars have been studying the collective creation of reality TV by producers, participants, and audiences. Attention has been paid to how the professionals, such as producers, advertisers, and distributors, contribute to the making of reality TV (Ouellette 2013). It has also been emphasized that "[t]he production, aesthetics and politics of reality TV are connected to audiences and publics, consumers and producers, participants and users, fans and anti-fans, readers, listeners, viewers—all these people and their practices" (Hill 2014: 7). Since "'access' and 'authenticity' are tenuous and contingent, created in an ongoing cultural struggle between producers, participants, and television viewers," the real is by no means a closed text over which the TV industry, part and parcel of the entire nexus of neoliberal institutions, has absolute control (Murray and Ouellette 2009: 12). It is worth highlighting that some scholars have attempted to locate indications of resistance in reality TV, an unstable text in which different enchantments are in competition and conflict.

The producers are indeed heavy-handed, taking control over prearrangement, editing, and reconstruction. The viewers, however, having been trained in the generic conventions of reality TV, are savvy and skeptical. They are always ready to "test out their own notions of the real, the ordinary, and the intimate against the representation before them ... and [create a] multilayered viewing experience that hinges on culturally and politically complex notions of what is real and what is not" (Murray and Ouellette 2009: 8). The participants in the shows are from this well-trained audience—just as Katniss is in *The Hunger Games*—and are thus equipped with the indispensable media literacy to perform themselves, while not necessarily conforming to the dictates of reality programing and the norms and values surrounding it (Latham and Hollister 2014). The reality boom is both a neoliberal instrument and an opportunity for ordinary people to wrestle with the culture industry and reappropriate television images and discourses.

The enchantment of reality TV cuts both ways. *The Hunger Games* show is no exception. In *The Hunger Games* novels/films, the show is a thoroughly commercialized state apparatus designed to train the citizens according to Panem's official ideologies, which combine state totalitarianism and neoliberal doctrines such as being self-enterprising and competing with others. The show, run by the state, receives sponsorship from the privileged class of the Capitol. It plays with the discourse of the real by reaping real children from the Districts, rather than using professional actors, and dumping them, after bare minimum training, into the arena to fight each other to the death. There is little scripting and directing involved, although the panoptic studio, or the arena, is carefully designed and meticulously monitored by the gamemakers, who cultivate dramatic uncertainties to excite the audiences. The entertaining real of *The Hunger Games* show is also the terrifying real. It is mass entertainment for the Capitol audience and a brutal public execution in the eyes of the District people.

The fictional show exercises the sovereign, disciplinary, and pastoral powers of Panem. First, its content is ritual sacrifice, the annual killing of twenty-three children to punish the Districts. Second, it allows one child to survive, promoting competitive individualism across Panem. It accustoms all Panem citizens to surveillance and turns them into docile bodies that regulate and manage themselves by fighting against competitors in the game of life beyond the arenas. Third, the show is pastoral in that it provides social welfare and offers lifestyle instructions.

The tesserae system attached to the games indicates that the show is charity-themed. Hungry children between twelve and eighteen can receive extra food from the government. However, their names will be entered into the reaping system an additional time. Most ironically, those who receive welfare from the state are more likely to be reaped into the fight. If we consider the makeover done by the team of stylists assigned to each tribute, the show is undeniably a lifestyle guide. One example is that in the film adaptation of *Catching Fire*, President Snow's granddaughter wears her hair in a braid like Katniss did in the 74th game and says that it is the popular fashion in her school.

Although a machine of enchantment controlled by Panem, *The Hunger Games* show is not a closed text but a playground for the complicated interaction between producers, participants, and audiences. The power of Panem does not dictate everything. The powerless have learned how to get by and even twist the show to their own advantage, as to be demonstrated in what follows.

4.2 The Hunger Games *Show: Nazi Camp and Disneyland*

In their analysis of *The Hunger Games* show as a political instrument deployed by Panem, Fani Cettl (2015) and Helen Day (2012) both examine the arena—the studio of the show. Cettl sees it as a reincarnation of the Nazi camp, where bare life is produced; Day argues that the arena is not unlike Disneyland, a fun place for the Capitol audience. Both the Nazi camp and the Disneyland park are where docile bodies are trained. Cettl contends that the show is a state-manufactured spectacle in service to a capitalist sovereignty that goes beyond the system of the nation-state. More specifically, "the fictional totalitarian nation-state's decision to isolate and kill bodies in the reality show can be read as an imagined radicalization of the current procedures and narratives in which young bodies are framed by the liberal competitive market" (Cettl 2015: 141). Similarly, Day points out that in the novels/films, the dominant Ideological State Apparatus of Panem, to use Louis Althusser's (1918–1990) terminology, is the media rather than the church or educational institutions. Along this line, I suggest that the official "church" of Panem, one that functions to promote and naturalize the totalitarian-capitalist ideologies of Panem, is *The Hunger Games* show.

Cettl and Day cite Guy Debord (1931–1994) and Jean Baudrillard (1929–2007) respectively, two theorists central to the discussion of reality TV. A brief introduction to Debord's "spectacle" and Baudrillard's "simulacrum" is in order.

What Debord means by spectacle is not the pre-modern spectacle of public torture and executions before the rise of disciplinary power. In *Society of the Spectacle* ([1967]1994), Debord presents spectacle as a phenomenon of late capitalism. It is the ultimate form taken by capitalism and essentially an image-mediated social relationship. A tool of pacification and depoliticization, it directs social subjects to see the world only by means of specialized mediations, freezes them in isolation from one another, and estranges them from genuine creative practices. For Debord, we live in a society of the spectacle organized around the production, circulation, and consumption of images. This society valorizes sight, the most abstract sense that corresponds to the abstraction of life under capitalism.

Influenced by Debord, Agamben emphasizes the role of modern media, especially television, in the production of bare life. In his 1967 book, Debord differentiated the "concentrated spectacle" associated with the Stalinist-type media and the "diffused spectacle" typical of the American consumer society. He later revised his thesis, arguing that these two fused into the integrated spectacle as a global sovereignty of the capitalist market began to eclipse that of the nation-state, although the latter was still relevant (Debord 1998). In *Means without End: Notes on Politics* (2000), Agamben takes up Debord's notion of the integrated spectacle and highlights television as playing a crucial role in this unification.

Although neither Debord nor Agamben discussed reality TV per se, Douglas Kellner counts it as one of the many media spectacles in our technocapitalist society where information and entertainment have merged. According to him, these media spectacles "embody contemporary society's basic values, serve to initiate individuals into its way of life, and dramatize its controversies and struggles, as well as its modes of conflict resolution" (Kellner 2003: 2). They are a new site for the production of the Durkheimian sacred. Baudrillard is the theorist who closely examined this new location. In *Simulacra and Simulation* (1994), he claims that media do not simply represent the real but simulate it—present a simulacrum of it. The simulated real of the screen consists of images, sounds, and texts. This version of the real, simulacrum, appears as no different from what we experience in everyday life. However, simulacrum is of a different order, which is named the hyperreal. The media, having produced this new level of reality that appears as such but cannot be confused with everyday life, play with these two orders, the real and the hyperreal.

Then comes reality TV, the apotheosis of simulacrum or the hyperreal. For Baudrillard, reality TV further complicates the hyperreality of TV because it conflates the real and the hyperreal, collapsing any distance between these two orders. While reality TV incorporates extra television reality en masse, the non-mediated extra television reality as such evaporates. In the era of reality TV, reality per se is always already replete with the interacting media and the incessant dissemination of information. What reality TV captures is a new level of media culture in which reality and hyperreality seamlessly blend inside and outside the space of the screen, whereas humans become human-machine interfaces or chimerical cocktails (Baudrillard 2005, 2011; Poster 2007). In this light, I view the Muttations, genetically engineered monsters that fuse humans and nonhumans, as the paradigmatic reality TV subjects.

Interestingly, Cettl and Day focus on the participants and viewers of the fictional reality show, respectively. Invoking Debord and Agamben, Cettl sees the arena as the Nazi camp and the show as a power mechanism that turns involuntary gamers like Katniss and Peeta into bare life. Following this line of thinking, I add that the show also exercises what Foucault and Agamben called bio-power beyond the arenas. Whereas disciplinary power produces the individual docile bodies, biopolitics manages entire populations. And, compared with the pastoral power that is pedagogical and spiritual, biopower is more targeted at biological issues such as reproduction and racial/species categorization. Two details of the show are worth mentioning: the reaping that kick-starts the show season is Panem's population census and the broadcast of the show targets the entire population.

For the population located in the Districts, the arena is indeed the nightmarish Nazi camp. However, for the Capitol fans of the show, the arenas from the previous games are popular vacation sites. The privileged citizens of the Capitol are those who "have a seemingly insatiable lust to become part of the spectacle and to involve themselves in it more intimately and peer into the private lives of others" (Kellner 2003: 19–20). As a result, they are obsessed with media-produced seductions and disconnected from socio-political and everyday realities. Day argues that the show is the hyperreality invented by the state of Panem and imposed onto the messy reality of its people. She regards the rationale of the show as to hijack the real, that is, to entertain the Capitol, disconnecting its citizens from the violence and repression everywhere, in addition to working as a "deterrence machine" to punish the Districts for their past rebellion against the Capitol. In this light, the arenas, where simulacra and the real are indistinguishable, are Panem's Disneyland, or at least the Capitol's. They are the circenses that accompanies Panem in the Latin phrase and the ideological blankets "covering ... the fact that violence and repression are everywhere" (Day 2012: 176).

In her article, Day believes that simulation is only a temporary state and that the hijacked real will eventually return. She sees real and not real as two distinct options, and the hyperreal as a stage in discovering a real, safer future.

Baudrillard would not agree with this reading. An "authentic" version of the real that is distinct from the hyperreal and always returns does not exist. Authenticity and artificiality are intertwined to such an extent that distinction between the two no longer makes sense. The only way out is to keep fighting within the games, which are not limited to the arenas or the fictional space of Panem.

4.3   The Unclosed Real and the Tactics of the Powerless

Katniss as a participant and viewer of *The Hunger Games* show is the center of much scholarly discussion, as presented by the works written by Rachel E. Dubrofsky and Emily D. Ryalls (2014), Catherine Driscoll and Alexandra Heatwole (2018: 28–34), Shannon R. Mortimore-Smith (2012), Connors (2014 b), and Katheryn Wright (2012).

Dubrofsky and Ryalls study Katniss in the film *The Hunger Games*, performed by Jennifer Lawrence, as a reality TV star who performs "non-performance" to win the favor of the audiences both within and outside the film. They argue that the film, not unlike the reality show within its fictional space, is an ideological apparatus set up to discipline and guide the individuals, or, more specifically, to perpetuate certain racial and gendered stereotypes. While surveillance in reality TV is an authenticating mechanism that follows the participants in a constructed setting to "confirm consistency of character across disparate spaces," the magic of a scripted film "is that it can fictionally represent life without cameras, in this case enabling the articulation of Katniss's consistent behavior across disparate spaces in ways a RTV show cannot" (Dubrofsky and Ryalls 2014: 398). Although Katniss's life in the film may or may not be subject to the gaze of Panem's surveillance cameras, the cameras of the film are not to be ignored. What is suggested is that the film is another show that frames *The Hunger Games* show. The authenticity of Katniss the character is a constructed fiction "premised on her authentic whiteness, her naturalized heterosexual femininity, and her effortless abilities to work as a potential future wife and mother" (Dubrofsky and Ryalls 2014: 407).

Driscoll and Heatwole also consider Katniss's authenticity as a reality TV star and a political figurehead in the novels/films. They acknowledge that the "performance of not-performing" discussed by Dubrofsky and Ryalls is key to Katniss's success. However, Driscoll and Heatwole point out that the cameras of the film are not always the extension of the reality TV cameras or the surveillance cameras of Panem. They highlight that "we never actually look at Katniss in the arena through the lens of a reality television program …[and that] we are firmly aligned with Katniss's experience rather than a televisual one, so that action is exclusively centered on Katniss rather than edited with cuts away to other contestants" (2018: 33). That is to say, the film is *both* an ideological apparatus through which the power of Panem (and our world) works *and* a field in which the struggle of the powerless leaves its traces. Resistance is not impossible inside and beyond the arenas.

Katniss's success, according to Mortimore-Smith, is not premised upon performing non-performance but in resisting the gaze of the audience, "to turn tables on the Capitol's rule and play 'Gamemaker' to her viewers' desires and demands" (2012: 165). Katniss and the other tributes are former viewers well-trained in the generic conventions and audience expectations of reality TV. In Mortimore-Smith's analysis, there are at least three moments in which Katniss frustrates the gaze of the viewers and seizes control of the game: her shooting an arrow into the judges' roast pig during the pre-game training, her respectful burial of Rue and salute to District 11, and her final attempt to commit double suicide with Peeta by swallowing a handful of poisonous berries.

Mortimore-Smith also draws a connection between the Capitol audience of Panem's reality show and the audiences of reality shows in the real-life world. In the novels/films (and beyond), the continuation of the show depends on the audience's insatiable desire for excitement, insensitivity to the suffering of the others, and active participation in the forms of voting and sponsorship. I add that these viewers not only internalize the disciplinary gaze of Panem but also help to strengthen that gaze when passionately following the show. To disrupt the gaze of the audience is to confront the sovereign, disciplinary, and pastoral powers of Panem. What is expected of the readers/viewers of the novels/films, as argued by Mortimore-Smith, is to learn how to practice critical reflection of their own spectatorship and to become conscientious participants in the making of the (hyper)real.

What the audiences inside and beyond Panem may want to learn is the tactics used by participants such as Katniss and Peeta. It is Connors who invokes Michel de Certeau's distinction of strategies and tactics (de Certeau 1984) to illustrate the limits of surveillance. Discontented with the metaphor of the panopticon, Connors refuses to see those subjects under the gaze as deprived of agency and incapable of resistance. Instead, he seeks to examine the peculiar and paradoxical outcomes of panoptic power, which is not monopolized by various disciplinary mechanisms but always susceptible to the creative manipulation of the weak. His attempt resonates with Jackson's endeavor to reconceptualize both religion and art as the various ways in which individuals in their everyday life process and appropriate the sacred. The tactics that de Certeau conceptualized are tactics of enchantment.

In *The Practice of Everyday Life* (1984), de Certeau studies the quotidian and seemingly insignificant maneuvers that ordinary people execute, such as how consumers play with the rules and resources that producers have imposed on them. He calls these maneuvers tactics and distinguishes them from strategies. For him, strategies are wielded by those in power who have access to an institutional space. The subject of strategies is able to use this space to store resources, make plans, and observe the less powerful, turning them into objects under surveillance. However, the weak subjects, forced to navigate themselves within structures beyond their own control, are not without power. They cunningly look for "cracks that particular conjunctions open in the surveillance of the proprietary powers" (de Certeau 1984: 37) and seize opportunities to turn those power apparatuses to their own advantage.

The arena is an institutional space where the gamemakers turn the tributes, or reality TV participants, into objects under surveillance. The entire country of Panem is a larger institutional space where the game of everyone against everyone is played. However, there are tactics within the show. In addition to Katniss's defiance as analyzed by Mortimore-Smith, Peeta has also learned to exploit the gaze of the cameras and the emotions of the audience. In Connors' reading, Peeta is a cunning participant who knows how to open up the fixed discourse of the real by manipulating the emotional responses of the audience. For instance, in a pre-game interview, Peeta confesses to the audience his love for Katniss, adding romance, another reality TV genre, to the gamedoc they are trapped in (Collins 2008: 130). After the 74th Hunger Games, Peeta publicly proposes to Katniss because President Snow suspects the authenticity of their relationship (Collins 2009: 73). Before the Quarter Quell, Peeta intentionally lies in another pre-game interview about Katniss's pregnancy, sending the audience into a rage over the inhumanity of the games and successfully undermining the legitimacy of the upcoming one (Collins 2009: 256).

It is to be added that even the producers are not always the subjects of strategies. Cinna, a stylist working for the reality show but secretly in support of the revolution, is good at smuggling submissive messages into the spectacle/ simulacrum of the show. The case in point is the wedding gown he designs for Katniss's pre-game interview under the specific directives of President Snow. When Katniss spins in front of the cameras, this white dress bursts into dark flames, transforming the obedient bride-to-be into the mockingjay, the symbol of revolution, the central image of a network of human-nonhuman forces, as discussed in the previous section.

Reality TV is not without a revolutionary potential. To substantiate this point, Wright (2012) turns to Walter Benjamin's essay "The Work of Art in the Age of Its Technological Reproducibility" ([1936] 2008), which observes how aesthetic experience and the meaning of art have changed under the conditions of new technology. The new technology in Benjamin's age was the cinema, which helped to bring about the shift from the cult value of an original work of art into the exhibition value of mass media and popular culture. In the fictional space of Panem that encapsulates our social reality, the new technology is television, or, more specially, reality TV as the apotheosis of TV. According to Wright, the exhibition value of the cinema has evolved into the participatory value that reality TV exemplifies. *The Hunger Games* show is a media event aimed to unite the disparate Districts and cultivate a mass audience that is emotionally responsive to the power of Panem.

Wright's reading echoes Debord's argument that the spectacle is an image-mediated social relationship that simultaneously unites people and keeps them in isolation from one another. However, Wright also sees *The Hunger Games* show as a site of aesthetic engagement where strategies meet tactics. Given the entanglement of religion and art, I argue that this site is *both* religious *and* artistic. The hyperreality of reality TV is an aesthetic construction involving producer strategies such as pre-scripting, camera movements, and editing choices. The tactics deployed by the powerless are primarily aesthetic too. In this light, Katniss is a performance artist "who composes what can only be considered art by using the seemingly crass and debased realism of reality television as a starting point" (Wright 2012: 103). What Wright focuses on is Katniss's burial of her ally Rue. Katniss decorates the dead girl's body with wild flowers and sings her the lullaby "The Meadow Song." While the sovereign power of Panem reduces them into bare life, Katniss's performative art restores their humanity. And, she performs right in front of the reality TV (and surveillance) cameras, which unwittingly broadcast her gesture of defiance to the national audience. Katniss succeeds in hijacking the show, transforming the indoctrination of Panem's official "church" into the religion/art of resistance for the oppressed.

4.4 *Rethinking Religion and Media in the Age of Reality TV*

The Hunger Games show, an institutional space governed by the sovereign, disciplinary, and pastoral powers of Panem and where the powerless people use tactics to put up tiny resistances, exemplifies the contestation over enchantment. Both the making of the spectacle/simulacrum and how it is taken up, glossed, and acted upon by producers, participants, and audiences are enchanting. In short, reality TV, whether explicitly featuring the theme of religion or not, does the religious/artistic work.

In their introduction to *Religion and Reality TV: Faith in Late Capitalism* (2018), Mara Einstein, Katherine Madden, and Diane Winston demonstrate that in the twenty-first century religion (or spirituality) has become a subgenre within reality TV and an ever-present theme in the ostensibly secular shows. Religious content proliferates in the reality genre on cable television and in digital media environments. The reality genre promotes the major themes of neoliberalism, such as the commercialization of the sacred and the management of the self. These themes constitute the lived religion of the audience, their everyday practices centered upon the quest for personal identity and the meaning and purpose of life. What is implied is that there is a religious dimension to neoliberalism and that this new religion/spirituality does not bother to limit itself within the boundaries of established religious traditions. And, the religion of neoliberalism takes reality TV as one of its institutions.

The Hunger Games show is both the state religion of Panem and the lived religion of its people. It is a church-like institution controlled by the state that represents global capitalism and the everyday struggle of the ordinary people. The struggle of life in the latter regard splits into a competitive and consumerist lifestyle promoted by the show and a loving attentiveness toward others and the world that disrupts the show from within. Repression and resistance are the two faces of enchantment. Moreover, religion and media are indistinguishable, attesting to Hent de Vries's thesis that the religious and the mediatic are mutually imbricated and even interchangeable within contemporary globalized societies (2001). De Vries believes that although religious traditions have always been entwined with and dependent upon media infrastructures, their relationship has become an intrinsic one under the contemporary conditions of technological advancements. As religion has become first and foremost a practice of mediation, scholars of religion should shift their attention "away from the bifurcation of faith and knowledge to the significance of the processes of mediation and mediatization without and outside of which no religion would be able to manifest or reveal itself in the first place" (de Vries 2001: 28). It is also because the media, as they have been supplementing and assuming roles of the state, have adopted some functions of religious institutions.

Although agreeing with de Vries that the impact of new technologies on religion cannot be ignored, Charles Hirschkind questions the theological assumptions implicit in de Vries' argument. To see religion as mediation presumes a post-Enlightenment Protestant theological perspective that looks for the (almost always imperfect) external expressions of (some authentic) internal religious experience. Instead, Hirschkind quotes Talal Asad, who has proposed that scholars of religion should examine the grammar of our social life "where psychological 'inside' and behavioral 'outside' are equally (though in different ways) signified by linguistic and nonlinguistic behavior that is publicly accessible" (Asad 2001: 139, quoted in Hirschkind 2011).

I find Hirschkind's critique fully convincing. "Interiorized" faith is indeed inseparable from "external" practices, institutions, and the circulation of sensibilities. Moreover, the supposedly pre-existing faith may very likely be a product of routinized, if not ritualized, actions. However, de Vries's thesis, although bogged down in his theological assumptions, may be helpful for us to study reality TV, where the Protestant internal-external divide is still at work. The voyeuristic desire for the authentic both presupposes some interiorized, or deeply buried, experience and demands it to be publicly displayed and made accessible to the audience. After all, the authentic must be performed. Only the behavioral outside is visible on the TV screen. On the one hand, the performance in reality TV is expected to be unmediated nonperformance—a "natural" expression of the internal in the external. On the other hand, the producers, participants, and audiences are all aware of the artificiality of the mediatic text they collectively construct. They do not simply practice mediation but play with the representation and fabrication of reality.

Similarly, religion, not unlike reality TV, is not so much a practice of mediation/mediatization as a game of mediation/mediatization defined by various sets of grammar. In its history of global spread and increasing aesthetic sophistication, reality TV has evolved to encompass a whole range of subgenres, all with their respective styles, rules, and audience expectations. Readers of *The Hunger Games* show have associated it with real-life reality shows such as *Big Brother, Survivor,* and *American Idol,* among many others. To assess the grammar of the state and lived religion of Panem, we need to consider the grammar of *The Hunger Games* show, which is a fusion of several subgenres—gamedoc, charity provider, lifestyle program, and not without a romantic element if we consider the "faked" relationship between Peeta and Katniss. More significant is the grammar of the game played by the producers, participants, and audiences—that is, the strategies of the powerful and the tactics of the powerless.

Studying gamedocs in particular, Nick Couldry argues that reality TV is ritualistic. By ritual he means "formalized action"—always more than it seems—"and action (often, but not necessarily, formalized) associated with certain transcendent values" (2009: 84). The second part of the definition clearly echoes Durkheim's definition of the sacred as the collective sentiments of a society. For Durkheim, ritual action is meant to affirm the values undergirding the social bond. Likewise, Couldry describes gamedocs as media rituals that "reproduce the building blocks of belief without involving any explicit content that is believed" (2009: 84).

Like Asad and Hirschkind, Couldry does not conceptualize ritual action as the externalization of some interiorized belief. Instead, media rituals bypass articulated beliefs to promote particular norms of behavior to discipline the human subjects. What is promoted is also the modern myth that the media are our privileged access point to social reality. As a media ritual, *The Hunger Games* show is not primarily concerned with indoctrinating the nationalist belief among its audiences. Instead, it cultivates obedience in the District bodies and a consumerist behavior in the Capitol bodies, with both sides taking the endless self-enterprising and cut-throat competition for survival for granted. What the show aims to maintain is the political, economic, and technological order of Panem as not only the sacred but also the single version of reality, and to establish itself as the only access point to that (hyper)reality. However, the entertaining and terrifying real of the show is not a closed text. In the struggle between multiple parties, participants/viewers such as Katniss and Peeta are able to enact their counter-enchantment. In this third space, this makeshift home, and a congruent moment of reality TV, the two types of enchantment surveyed in the first two sections are interlocked, although violently opposed and mutually exclusive. Their contestation extends beyond the arenas and the TV network into the everyday life of Panem centered upon food and clothing, the primary concern of the next section.

5 The Split Enchantment of Food and Clothing, the Game of Hungers

While the Hunger Games are fought within the arenas and broadcast as *The Hunger Games* reality show, a game of hungers over food and clothing is the everyday reality of Panem. In the Districts, the physical hunger triggered by the bare minimum of food and clothing dominates. In the Capitol, the extravagance of gourmet food and high fashion cultivates a hunger for amoral excitement. In both cases, food and clothing serve as instruments of domination. Resistance against Panem also takes up these objects, material and symbolic, as weapons. Scholarship on *The Hunger Games* novels/films has already turned to the relevant fields for analytical tools. In this section, I offer a brief overview of food studies and fashion studies, paying particular attention to the theorizations developed by Roland Barthes (1915–1980), Baudrillard, and Bourdieu. Next, I summarize and comment on scholarship analyzing the depiction of food and clothing in the novels/films. The study of religion, food, and clothing, or, more precisely, the material turn in the study of religion, is the primary concern of the last part of this section. In this section, I endeavor to argue that food and clothing in Panem are the organizing center of everyday life, which is a game of split enchantment, repressive and liberatory, not unlike the reality show discussed in the previous section and the transmedia universe, the subject of the sixth and last section.

5.1   Food and Clothing: Foodways and Fashion Systems

Food and clothing are essentials of life that shape our embodiment. They are material and symbolic, universal and particular, basic life sustenance and the center of ideas, practices, and organizations. The study of food and that of clothing are relatively new fields that have been experiencing rapid growth for three decades. Scholars take multidisciplinary approaches to food and clothing, which, seemingly quotidian and insignificant, are highly charged sites where the complex relationships between the body, individual and collective identities, and large-scale discourses and institutions are played out.[9]

The intake of food and the wearing of clothes, vital to human survival, seem to be universal practices but actually bear marks of socio-cultural difference. Among the distinct traits differentiating one group from another we can always count food habits and clothing decisions. In the field of food studies, a frequently used term is foodway, which, according to Kathleen C. Riley and Amy L. Paugh, "covers *all* the material and symbolic ways in which humans 'do food' in both everyday and formal settings. In other words, it includes how we grow, cook, exchange, store, eat, compost, and communicate through, about, and around food, constructing both actual food as well as the notion of nourishment" (2018: 5). Riley and Paugh further describe "doing food" as a multisensual experience like language. Habits of both are embodied forms of knowledge and practice acquired through everyday social interactions. Agendas of both are to bind or separate communities, to resolve or escalate conflicts across boundaries (Riley and Paugh 2018: 1–4).

What corresponds to foodway is fashion in a broad sense. In fashion studies, fashion is defined as a system encompassing the discrete clothing items, the practices to wear them, and much more. Used in a broad sense, fashion refers to an entire set of thoughts and actions centered upon adorning the body with clothes. In a narrow sense, scholars such as Elizabeth Wilson (1987) and Joanne Entwistle (2000) have argued that fashion is not a transhistorical or transcultural system but a product of the capitalist modern West, although it has been democratized and globalized to a limited extent. A system defined by regular and rapid change, fashion is enmeshed in capitalist relations of production and consumption and located in societies where social mobility is possible.

---

9   For an introduction to food studies, see Counihan et al. 1997; Albala 2019. For fashion studies, see Craik 1994; Entwistle 2000.

Furthermore, Agnès Rocamora and Anneke Smelik describe fashion as "a commercial industry producing and selling material commodities; a sociocultural force bound up with the dynamics of modernity and postmodernity; and an intangible system of signification" (2015: 1). They acknowledge that this system "is ... made of things and signs, as well as individual and collective agents, which all coalesce through practices of production, consumption, distribution and representation" (2015: 1). Likewise, the anthropological category of foodway in a broad sense is supplemented by the much narrower notion of food industry. For instance, Marion Nestle has demonstrated how public opinions regarding what to eat are shaped by the commercial industry of food, with food companies seeking to coopt nutritional research and influence governmental agencies (2013).

With regard to the symbolic dimension of foodways and fashion systems, especially their industrialization under capitalism, the theorist par excellence is Barthes, a semiotician who was primarily interested in how food and clothing are articulated in words and images. For him, a symbolic system is endowed with internal rules or grammars and open to interpretations and appropriations. Located in symbolic systems, food and clothing items have a communicative dimension that is even mythical. His seminal essay "Toward A Psychosociology of Contemporary Food Consumption" argues that food is "not only a collection of products that can be used for statistical or nutritional studies ...[but] also, at the same time, a system of communication, a body of images, a protocol of usages, situations, and behavior" (1997: 21).

Likewise, Barthes's *The Fashion System* ([1967]1983) studies the fashion magazine as a generator of fashion by applying the techniques of structural linguistics to fashion-clothing, or, more precisely, written clothing and image-clothing. According to him, clothing is first and foremost a sign or a text. It is a function-sign, consisting of the testamentary code, the terminological code, and the rhetorical code—that is, actual garments classified according to their production and consumption, words in spoken language to designate these garments, and verbal and visual representations of clothing in fashion editorials and spreads (Barthes 1983; Jobling 2015). Since the novels and films of *The Hunger Games* are verbal and visual representations of both food and clothing, no wonder Barthes is frequently quoted in relevant scholarship.

Another scholar applying the structuralist linguistic methodology to the study of food and clothing is Baudrillard, who analyzed McDonald's hamburgers and Levi's jeans in books such as *The Consumer Society: Myths and Structures* (1998) and *Symbolic Exchange and Death* (2017). Going beyond Barthes's structuralist semiotics, he focused on the postmodern age, arguing that signs, having been emptied of their meanings, refer only to other signs in the same system, not any external signifieds. In this non-signifying age, food or clothing is no longer primarily life sustenance or a form of communication. Pleasure is the ultimate goal. What Baudrillard meant by postmodern fashion is a playful spectacle, a carnival of appearances, and an extravagant waste of society's excess. He also surveyed how signification worked in premodern and modern societies. Using his periodization, Efrat Tseëlon explains the changing meanings of clothes as imitation in the premodern world, production as linked to modernity, and postmodern simulation and seduction (2015).

More specifically, in the premodern period, when signs were meant to mirror the social order, clothes were worn to create discrimination from nature and regulate proper distance between bodies. In the modern world, the premodern tie between the signifier and the signified or appearance and reality began to break; clothes no longer referred unequivocally to status. This is because the mass production of clothes made fashion trickle down from higher to lower classes and opened a struggle for meaning. Meanwhile, the use value of clothes transformed into the exchange value of consumer goods; utility was replaced by symbolism. In the postmodern age, the indirect link between the signifier and signified eventually dissolves. What dominates this era are the links between the signifier and the signifier, links that subvert signification and negate the seriousness of reality, morality, and meaning. Postmodern fashion is not so much a matter of form and style as a perpetual play of the empty signs, which refer to nothing but themselves. A perfect case in point is the fashionable life of the Capitol, or, more specifically, *The Hunger Games* reality program as a makeover show.

The third theorist worthy of our attention is Bourdieu, who agreed with Barthes and Baudrillard that food and clothing exist not only as actual objects but also through discourses on them. However, while Barthes and Baudrillard merely read actual objects in relation to these discourses on them, Bourdieu argued that these objects and discourses function within a wider system of production called "the field." In *The Field of Cultural Production: Essays on Art and Literature* (1993), he explains the field, exemplified by the literary field, as a social microcosm encapsulating various agents and institutions as well as their practices and interactions governed by specific rules. In a field, meanings and values are not inherent in objects—such as food items, clothes, or works of literature and the arts—but determined by the state of power relations (that is, the structure of the field) at a particular time and place.

It is worth highlighting that what Bourdieu meant by production, echoing Barthes, is more symbolic than material, cultural than economic. However, Rocamora argues that it does not imply that Bourdieu, a Marxist, wished to ignore the production of commercial goods and the social relations built upon this production (2015). In her interpretation of Bourdieu, she emphasizes that for him, a field is made up of unequal positions, and one's position is determined by the various types of capital one holds. Struggles in a field are struggles to determine the legitimate forms of capital and their composition. Bourdieu distinguished four types of capital. In addition to economic capital held by an agent or institution, there are also social, symbolic, and cultural capitals. Social capital refers to one's social contacts and networks; symbolic capital, one's status; cultural capital, the set of cultural resources embodied in manners, objectified as books or works of art, or institutionalized in certificates like diplomas. Among the four, economic capital is the root and can be converted into the other three. Eventually, all these types of capital can be embodied.

Embodied capital is external wealth converted into a person's habitus, defined in *The Logic of Practice* as "schemes of perception, appreciation and action ... acquired through practice and implemented in the practical state without attaining explicit representation" (Bourdieu 1990: 95). In a particular field, agents seek to maximize their profit while exhibiting an incorporated disposition dictated by their habitus, which is produced by the successive generations in a particular type of condition of existence. On this basis, Bourdieu argues in *Distinction: A Social Critique of the Judgement of Taste* (2000) that aesthetic experience is a socially and historically constituted disposition, in contrast to Kant's conceptualization of aesthetic experience as an independent and universal expression of the mind.

According to Bourdieu, culture is a vector of social distinctions, tastes are markers of class, and habitus is embodied capital. The enchantment story told in *The Hunger Games* novels/films is also one of distinction. The privileged dwellers of the Capitol and the working class of the Districts, due to abundance or lack of economic capital in their respective lives, have radically different embodied habits and aesthetic tastes. The bourgeoisie, equipped with economic and other capitals, enjoy the luxurious, while the workers only have a taste for what they can afford and what is useful and functional. However, that is only one side of the story. The complex role played by food and clothing in *The Hunger Games* novels/films is to be examined.

5.2   *Food and Clothing: The Game of Hungers beyond the Arenas*

Since food and clothing populate representational structures such as literature, film, and the other arts, subfields such as literary food studies[10] and fashion

---

10   For recent scholarship on literature and food, see Boyce and Fitzpatrick 2017; Tigner and Carruth 2017; Piatti-Farnell and Brien 2018; Lorna and Brien 2018.

and fiction[11] have emerged. Studying food and clothing, scholars have made extensive use of literary sources, both imaginary literature and vernacular food/fashion writings such as cookery books, dietary literature, fashion magazines, and catalogue descriptions. Moreover, particular attention has been paid to how food and clothing are enacted in literary/filmic texts. When specific food items and how they are consumed are described in fictional texts, or when the same authors take pains to depict garments and accessories, the reader knows that the items represented speak for themselves and carry messages beyond themselves.

These items/words help to build characters, illustrating their social standings, personal idiosyncrasies, and relationships with other people. They also indicate the progression of the plot or directly propel the unfolding of events. Furthermore, they add substance to the imagined world of a fictional text and make possible alternative explorations other than getting to know the characters or following how the plot unfolds. The stories of food and clothing even extend beyond a given text. They are potent, protean, and multi-faceted symbols embedded in the larger texts of human histories, telling stories of power and poverty, labor and leisure, individuality and collectivity. The invocation of these symbols is not just a mere reflection of real-life ideas and practices; literary/filmic texts through enacting food and fashion help to shape the non-fictional discourses on them.

Much ink has been spilled on food and clothing in *The Hunger Games* novels/films. In what follows I introduce how Max Despain (2012), Meghan Gilbert-Hickery (2016), Jem Bloomfield (2017), and Lori L. Parks and Jennifer P. Yamashiro (2015) have discussed food, and how Christina van Dyke (2012), Deirdre Bryne (2015), and Amy L. Montz (2012, 2016) have worked on the fictional representation of clothing. These scholars have collectively presented the handling of food and clothing as *both* the strategies of Panem's disciplinary and pastoral power *and* the tactics of the ordinary people who hunger for a decent life, social justice, and personal freedom. Beyond the arenas of the games and the screens of reality TV, a game of enchantment, disenchantment, and re-enchantment is perpetually played by the entire nation of Panem.

One of the first scholars to study food in *The Hunger Games* novels, Despain sees food as a marker of class distinction. He contrasts the abundance of food in the Capitol with the scarcity of it in the Districts. Food is "a political and cultural status symbol" in the Capitol and an indispensable means for personal

---

11 For discussion of fashion as enacted in print literature and audio-visual media, see McNeil, Karaminas, and Cole 2009.

survival and community making in the Districts (Despain 2012: 70). The banquet after the Victory Tour in *Catching Fire* is used as an example to illustrate the former point. At the banquet, partygoers eat for the sake of eating. They have to regurgitate again and again in order to stuff themselves with the delicacies on display. The author's inspiration may come from the popular myth of the Roman "vomitorium," a place set aside for ancient Romans to vomit in so as to make room for more food. In light of Baudrillard's discussion of the non-signifying postmodern signs, I revise Despain's thesis by suggesting that food symbolizes status only when the Capitol is contrasted with the Districts, with the opulent and meager food proportions corresponding to privilege and poverty, respectively. Within the Capitol, food is no longer a status symbol but an empty sign. Capitol dwellers indulge in playing with the gastronomic excess and piling upon themselves dazzling fabrics, while watching the spectacular ritual sacrifice in the format of a reality show, around which an entire array of feasts and fashion shows evolves.

By contrast, food in the Districts is scarce, so that people there are busy with keeping themselves alive and hence not able to rebel against the Capitol. However, procuring food brings people together. It helps to build group solidarity for the sake of survival. "Each outlying district in Panem forms an identity around not only the products the district is known for but also the ways in which its citizens cope with their lack of food" (Despain 2012: 70). In District 12, Katniss, with the help of her friend Gale, practices illegal hunting and trade to provide for her family. Despain reads her partnership with Gale as a crucial step toward community making. While this step exhibits her independence and ingenuity, there is also help from Peeta, who throws burnt bread to her, inviting her to embrace a more domestic and stable type of social bond. Food helps to connect people from within each District as well as across the divides of different Districts. Examples are the bread sent to Katniss from District 11 after the burial ritual she performs for Rue (Collins 2008: 238–239) and the different types and numbers of bread rolls sent to the tributes within the Quarter Quell as secret codes regarding the rebellion (Collins 2009: 385).

For Gilbert-Hickey, food, especially the bread, is not so much a mark of distinction as a link between the different classes and genders. She invokes Barthes, who stressed the communicative significance of food, brings up Bourdieu's concept of the habitus, and quotes de Certeau, who claimed that bread "remains the indelible witness of a 'gastronomy of poverty': it is less a basic food than a basic 'cultural symbol,' a monument constantly restored to avert suffering and hunger" (1998: 86, quoted in Gilbert-Hickey 2016: 99). Focusing on the bread, Gilbert-Hickey studies its role as "an incentive for various kinds of relationship-making in the trilogy" (2016: 98).

The bread divides and unites people along various lines. Class is one of them. Reviewing the scene in which Katniss and Peeta dine with Effie Trinket, the escort of tributes from District 12, on the train to the Capitol, Gilbert-Hickey notices that when Trinket gives them training on table manners, she comments that the two kids last year "ate everything with their hands like a couple of savages" (Collins 2008: 44). Katniss boldly defends them, arguing that manners do not matter for those who barely have enough to eat. What is illustrated is Bourdieu's notions of class distinction and embodied habitus. More interestingly, Gilbert-Hickey calls our attention to what Peeta does to defy those table manners. He surreptitiously dips bits of bread in hot chocolate to start a seemingly insignificant rebellion in which Katniss quickly participates. Although de Certeau is quoted, the author does not mention his discussion of tactics, for which the dipping bread episode is a perfect example.

Another tactic in the novels is the slipping of bread that brings people from different classes together. Octavia, a member of Katniss's prep team from the Capitol, gives Katniss a piece of bread to make friends with her. Later in District 13, where strict food rationing is enforced, she steals an additional slice of bread and is severely punished as a result (Collins 2010: 48). Her predicament, together with many other incidents, makes Katniss realize that District 13 is no different from the Capitol, neither allowing people to break rules or form subgroups. The slice of bread from Octavia communicates a lot to Katniss, who eventually assassinates President Coin to prevent the rise of another totalitarian regime.

In addition to class, gender is a construct that bread reinscribes and destabilizes. Gilbert-Hickey stresses that bread does not separate but connects the two genders. Katniss is the hunter and later the face of revolution active in the political realm, while Peeta, the boy with the bread, plays a nurturing feminine role in the domestic sphere. The story ends with the marriage of these two non-stereotypical characters. By contrast, the ultra-feminine Prim dies rescuing children from the bombs Gale has designed; the ultra-masculine Gale leaves Katniss for a career-driven lonely life. What Gilbert-Hickey learns from Collins's story is that "rigid gender norms don't work and will, in the end, prove to be an insurmountable detriment" (2016: 101).

Among scholars scrutinizing the interplay of food in *The Hunger Games* novels/films, Bloomfield duly notes the overlap of the symbolic system of food and that of Christianity. In his own words, he is "not suggesting that Collins wrote this book as an exploration of eucharistic themes within a dystopian future, nor that she 'hid' a Christian 'message' inside her novel. There is nonetheless a powerful strain of imagery which maps so strongly over familiar symbols and themes within the Christian tradition, that it demands attention" (2017:

194). More specifically, he relates the first novel's engagement with the question of social inclusion and solidarity to gospel themes and contrasts the re-enchantments of the Christian tradition and postmodern consumer culture in the allegedly disenchanted modern world.

Like the other scholars, Bloomfield recognizes the significance of bread as the sustenance of life, means of political control, and glue that builds and maintains group identity. His contribution is that his reading reminds us that the symbol of food does the religious/artistic work of enchantment as theorized by Jackson, Morgan, and Chidester. He considers Peeta's effort to help Katniss, by tossing her burnt bread, a metaphorical "burnt offering," an image of sacrifice in the Hebrew Bible. The bread sent to Katniss from District 11 is also a sacrifice meant to unite people across the divided boundaries of the Districts. These little sacrifices directly challenge the sacrifice demanded by Panem discussed in section 1. In response to the sacrificial bread offered by District 11, Katniss improvises a ritual of thanksgiving, in which "she uses a word which in NT Greek appears as 'eucharistia' and is paralleled with 'blessing' in the accounts given of the Last Supper by 2 Corinthians and the Gospel of Matthew" (Bloomfield 2017: 194).

The religious dimension of the symbol of food has also been noticed by other scholars. Despain discusses the lamb stew that Katniss names as her favorite during a pre-game interview. The lamb is a symbol of the Capitol's power over the tributes, including Katniss, who is like the sacrificial lamb slaughtered for the stew (Despain 2012). Working along the same line, Parks and Yamashiro read the *The Hunger Games* novel/film as a grand-scale *memento mori* image. Vanitas or *memento mori* is a low-ranking subgenre in still-life paintings in seventeenth-century Europe. These paintings "represent the passage of time, the vanity of earthly pleasures, and transience of life ...[and] celebrate the material world by displaying commodities from simple necessity to sumptuous luxuries to assuage terror by the splendor of the scene, a feast for the eyes and the senses" (Parks and Yamashiro 2015: 139). Analyzing the images of various food items, Parks and Yamashiro demonstrate that the novel and the film tap into the art historical convention of *memento mori* to depict the terror and splendor of Panem.

Compared with food, clothing is a no less fascinating topic in *The Hunger Games* literature. Earlier I introduced that there are two definitions of fashion, one identifying it as a universal system, the other taking it as a modern, Western, and capitalist construct. The second definition prevails in the articles I survey here, which see fashion as existing only in the Capitol. Van Dyke links food and fashion to the biopolitics of Panem. In her reading, people of the Districts struggle to satisfy their hunger for food, while the citizens of the Capitol organize their lives around satisfying their hunger for fashion and entertainment. Put together, the two sides form the so-called *"panem et circenses."* People living in the Districts are burdened with a daily struggle for food and have no time, energy, or resources to put up resistance against the Capitol. For the Capitol citizens, their bodies are disciplined to fit certain social norms. More specifically, they are trained to be self-centered, self-enterprising individuals, practicing self-surveillance and self-correction. They pursue frivolous fashion and the immoral entertainment of *The Hunger Games* show to keep themselves away from thinking about, not to mention challenging, social injustice (van Dyke 2012).

Like van Dyke, Sullivan endorses the narrow definition of fashion. He makes a distinction between fashion and dress. According to Entwistle (2000), dress, which designates the activity of clothing, adorning, and/or modifying the body, is more often used in anthropological literature that studies human cultures and societies in general. In other words, the term *dress* is closer to the broad definition of fashion. The act of dressing not only has a material dimension but also plays symbolic, communicative, and aesthetic functions. Entwistle also explains that, when considered in relation to fashion in the modern West, dress means the translation, or the concrete embodiment, of fashion. Fashion provides not only the garments but also the discourses around them, both to be translated into everyday dressing practices. Social factors such as class, race, and gender are entangled with the aesthetic ideas propagated by fashion to frame the practice of dressing, which marks out these categories of difference on the body.

I point out that Sullivan makes no reference to Entwistle's conceptualization of dress. For Sullivan, dress refers to the garments, the practices of dressing, and the discourses underlining those practices in the Districts. Dress is the non-fashionable "fashion" system of the Districts. Echoing van Dyke, Sullivan sees fashion as only for the elites in the Capitol, a tiny minority, and associates dress, defined as garments for protection, warmth, and utility, with the workers of the Districts. Emphasizing the class distinction between fashion and dress, he argues that the novels/films undermine our understanding of fashion as something already democratized.

Analyzing the movies based on the novels, Sullivan sees the urban flâneurs "who live among the ultra-modern glittering glass and steel skyways of Capitol ... [and are] clad in a spectacular array of fashioned excess ... [which] draws on the extremes of eighteenth-century baroque and rococo styles, as well as more recent outlandish subcultural fashions and fads" (2014: 185). This vivid illustration of the Baudrillardian postmodern fashion, a carnival of empty signs, stands in stark contrast to scenes of the Districts. The workers there wear sober, practical, and roughly hewn clothes, embodying moments such as the Great Depression and World War II in the 1930s and 1940s. District 12, where Katniss is from, is described as "a mythical place somewhere between Steinbeck's dust bowl and Springsteen's rust belt, and given a set redolent of Orwell's *1984* (Radford, 1984) and the rail yard scenes in Spielberg's *Schindler's List* (1993)" (Sullivan 2014: 184).

The divide between function and fashion, or the Districts and the Capitol, the central concern of Bryne's paper, is not only classed but also gendered, with the former marked masculine and the latter feminine. The point she makes is that women and men experience bodily regulations differently. "Women's identities are interwoven with corporeality in particularly intense ways; for this reason, they are the primary economic and discursive targets of the clothing and fashion industries" (Bryne 2015: 47). Before modernity, Tertullian, an early church father, saw women as the devil's gateway and took pains to write about how women should dress themselves, without giving any regard to what men should wear. In the nineteenth century, the most obvious gendered split in Western dress came about—the divide between trousers for men and skirts for women. The divide is still in place in the fictional Panem.

Bryne observes that Katniss, the hunting girl in trousers, is forced by the state to wear feminine dresses and become a docile body. Bryne also points out that the utilitarian clothes of the Districts (what Sullivan would call "dress") are markedly masculine, whereas the decorative, frivolous clothes of the Capitol (Sullivan's "fashion") are perceived as feminine. The masculine is the downtrodden striving for survival; the feminine is associated with the decadent privileged. "In addition, Katniss's hunting outfit sports more natural colors than the garish, highly-styled Capitol fashions: it combines masculine functionality with feminine references to nature" (Bryne 2015: 53). What Bryne endeavors to critique is that the novels/films unwittingly reinscribe Tertullian's misogynistic view of ornamentation, or fashion, as corrupt, unnatural, and womanly in an improper way.

Both Bryne and van Dyke question the one-dimensional view of fashion as corrupt excess. The latter further demonstrates the potential of fashion to reflect and deflect the gaze and to create possibilities for symbolic resistance in spectacular forms. For van Dyke, fashion is both a biopolitical tool to discipline the docile bodies and an effective means of self-expression and resistance against the dominant structure of power, because, per Foucault, power is more a matter of fluid and productive relations than a fixed asset or capacity possessed and exercised by one group over another. And, I assert that the enchantment of the ordinary people's lived religion is not always overwhelmed by the enchantment of Panem's state religion. The enchantment of fashion is indeterminant. Both van Dyke and Bryne analyze how Cinna, Katniss's stylist, designs for her the mockingjay outfit, branding her a hybrid like the bird, partly programmed by the state, partly wild—that is, beyond human control. While fashion as a biopolitical tool serving Panem is like the bioengineered jabberjay, fashion in the hands of the rebels is not unlike the mockingjay, the hybrid offspring of the jabberjay and the mockingbird (see the discussion of the mockingjay in section 2).

Katniss is the mockingjay, her body fashioned by the Capitol and then the rebels, both fully cognizant of the power of physical presentation and public spectacle. Acknowledging that fashion is a language written especially on the bodies of women, Montz notices that neither Panem nor the resistance against it is willing to hand this language over to women, who are merely bodies to be written on, not hands that write. While Panem deploys this language to control its people, the rebels re-appropriate it and create their own spectacle. The two spectacles are both feminized and passive. The gaze, by contrast, is masculine and aggressive. The gender politics of Panem and that of the rebellion are the same. It is true that Cinna sends political messages by dressing Katniss. However, Montz highlights that although the political messages of the Capitol and the rebels may contrast each other, they practice the same type of material discipline of women's bodies (2012).

In Montz's analysis, Katniss always embodies someone else's definition of the mockingjay. It is not until toward the end of the trilogy, after her assassination of President Coin and then solitary confinement, that she bursts out singing after a long silence and becomes the mockingjay on her own terms. Katniss the singer at that moment is the real rebel. She has learned to negotiate between the inner desire—hunger for freedom, justice, and beauty—and the various constrains imposed on her from the outside. This existential struggle is the work of religion and art and the root of genuinely radical politics. The disciplined docile body, or the disposable bare life, by pursuing the work of religion/art, may be able to refashion and empower herself in and against the world dominated by material difficulties and hostile forces.

5.3   *Food, Clothing, and the Material Turn in the Study of Religion*

Having introduced the current literature on food and clothing in *The Hunger Games* novels/films, I point out that only a few articles on food have made explicit references to religion (Despain 2012; Parks and Yamashiro 2015; Bloomfield 2017). Emphasizing the symbolic dimension of food, these articles treat religion (or, more specifically, Christianity) as a symbolic system, attesting to the influence of Barthes and Baudrillard on the one hand, and Clifford Geertz (1926–2006) on the other. While Barthes and Baudrillard traced how material objects worked within symbolic systems, Geertz defined religion as "a system of symbols which acts to establish powerful, pervasive, and long-lasting moods in men by formulating conceptions of a general order of existence and clothing those conceptions with such an aura of factuality that the moods and motivations seem uniquely realistic" (1973: 91). The attention paid to the symbolic dimension of material things and phenomena marks the material turn in the study of religion.

Although the question of religion is conspicuously absent in articles that analyze how fashion in both broad and narrow senses is portrayed in the novels/films, these articles have all emphasized how Panem uses clothing (and food) as a strategy to discipline the human body. In this regard, if we follow Asad to redefine religion as first and foremost a matter of bodily discipline (2009), the story told by the novels/films turns out undeniably religious, while the analysis of the disciplinary power of fashion also helps us to see fashion as doing religious and artistic work at the same time. As mentioned in the previous section, Asad does not take material things and embodied practices as external expressions of pre-existing beliefs. Instead, their goal is to discipline human subjectivity within networks of power. What resonates with Asad is Chidester's emphasis on the two materialities of religion: the material stuff of religion and the material conditions of various power structures.

It is worth noting that all these articles see food and clothing as sites for the enchantment of Panem's bodily discipline and the counter-enchantment of the ordinary people's tactics, again inevitably embodied. The former makes and maintains the sacred, while the latter, in Jackson's language, helps individuals in everyday situations to reappropriate collective representations that have become fixed and repressive, or even to debunk and rebuild these representations. In other words, the latter is able to disenchant and re-enchant the sacred for the sake of the sacrificed. In the game of hungers, there is also the hunger for personal freedom and social justice. The embodied experience or consciousness is not only Jackson's central category of analysis but also the foundation of resistance in the novels/films. Likewise, Morgan attends to the interaction of the human subject with the external material world. He defines religion as a form of sensation: it is experienced through various senses, which are fundamentally bodily processes at both individual and collective levels (2010, 2012).

The three lines of scholarly inquiries presented above overlap with the three main approaches in the material turn in the study of religion as summarized by Sonia Hazard: 1) Geertz's symbolic definition of religion and the treatment of material things and practices as religious symbols, 2) Asad's emphasis on bodily discipline in relation to power and the study of how material disciplines shape religious subjects and traditions, and 3) Morgan's conceptualization of religion as bodily sensations and the study of the inflection of material things in human senses and sensibilities as religious (2013). Hazard critiques the strong inclination toward anthropocentrism in all three approaches and identifies the fourth approach as a new materialism that studies how things operate beyond the horizons of human senses. I find a similar inclination toward anthropocentrism in existing scholarship on food and clothing in the novels/films, which has not yet viewed those material objects on their own terms. Although Morgan has already tried to locate the agency of enchantment in the network of human and nonhuman actants and to open up new terrains for the study of material religion (2018), more work needs to be done on the enchantment of food and clothing from a nonanthropomorphic perspective.

That said, the material turn, referring to "the claim of material things and phenomena—objects, practices, spaces, bodies, sensations, affects, and so on—to a place at the center of scholarly inquiry" (Hazard 2013: 59), has already destabilized the modern, Western, and Protestant category of religion. Although not all religious traditions marginalize the practices of eating and dressing, the post-Enlightenment model of religion does not reserve much space for them. When religion is defined as interiorized piety in some otherworldly transcendent power, everyday practices of feeding and adorning the body in a material world are pushed outside the boundaries of proper religion. It takes time for scholars to rediscover food and clothing, which have never been absent from religious traditions, many of which have rules about how food should be produced, prepared, and consumed and how to dress the bodies to maintain social order and civilizational identity. There are also rituals involving special food offerings and ritualistic attires.

It is without doubt that there are tendencies to denounce the material objects of food and clothing and the "dangerous" symbolic meanings they carry. For instance, as Elizabeth Pérez (2016) points out, Christian moral teachings, followed by classical Enlightenment texts, attached negative connotations to appetite, among other sensations, and put taste at the very bottom of the sensory hierarchy. While gustatory events were excluded from the ranks of experiences able to deliver a morally valuable encounter with the sacred, this exclusion was inseparable from the modern, Western, and Christian condemnation of indigenous traditions from the other (that is, colonized) parts of the world. These traditions were viewed as "superstitious" because they valorized "false" idols and "improper" forms of worship including food preparation and dressing practices.

The relationship between religion and fashion (in the narrow sense) is even more tensive. The Christian tradition is not without its ascetic aspects, condemning the material, sensual body together with the food and attire it needs. To make things worse, there is a secularist discourse that valorizes fashion as a favorite child of capitalism and dismisses religion as repressive of human needs. Religion and fashion are posited as polarities. Fashion values and accentuates the beauty of the human body, whereas Christian moral teachings tend to spite and denigrate the sensual, worrying about the corruptions of the sinful body. And, the female body is particularly charged. Entwistle (2000) reminds us that in much eighteenth- and nineteenth-century social theory, the body was still closely associated with women and pushed to the margins of society. Hence, women in fashion are seen as liberated agents of their own self-determined paths of fulfillment. By contrast, women who dress modestly for religious reasons are viewed as passive victims of sexist, patriarchal traditions.

In sum, the body and by extension the material world in general are closely associated with women, the lower classes, and the "primitive" non-whites—the very margins of the privileged human subject. In the modern world, the irruption of all these others grounds the reevaluation of food and clothing. While some religious orthodoxies condemn the indulgence in food and fashion, there is also a secular orthodoxy that elevates fashionable women and gastronomic pleasure and reduces religion to the mental, the spiritual, and the abstract. What is lost in the two contrasting types of orthodoxies is the one and same materiality of religion.

The material turn brings items of food and clothing, located in foodways and fashion systems, among many other objects, practices, and sensations, back around so as to renew our understanding of religion. Much work has been done to bring to light the connections between religious traditions, foodways, and fashion systems.[12] Emerging from these projects is a new model of religion as the everyday practices of the ordinary people, not always dictated by established institutions, doctrinal teachings, and religious elites (McGuire 2008). It has also been argued that, for these people, religion is not a matter of peculiar beliefs preoccupied with some fantasy land elsewhere, but has everything to do with relationships among human beings themselves and between the human and nonhuman. Here the nonhuman, or the sub- and/or super-human, may or may not be identified as the transcendent, the supernatural, or the sacred (G. Harvey 2013).

---

12   For religion and food, see Piatti-Freeley-Harnik 1995; Sack 2000; Madden 2006; Zeller 2014; Plate 2014. For religion and fashion, see Lewis 2013, 2015; Eicher and Hume 2013.

The old forms of organized religion have been shrinking in the contemporary world, in which new actors are drawing on new resources and technologies to modify traditional beliefs and practices and make new forms of association. Women are among these new actors. They now operate outside organized religion and work to reclaim religion, which is no longer defined as the extraordinary, sublime, or other-worldly. Moreover, I call for more attention paid to non-Western religious traditions, which, despite their low status in Eurocentric classificatory schemes, are rich depositories of resources worthy of exploration because they often value food and clothing as crucial links between the human and the divine. Although we may have difficulty aligning the split enchantment as depicted in *The Hunger Games* novels/films with the modern, Western, and Protestant model of religion, other models of religion may help us to make sense of the Hunger Games, *The Hunger Games* show, and the game of hungers beyond the arenas/screens.

6 The Split Enchantment of *The Hunger Games* Transmedia Assemblage

The Hunger Games is a reality show located at the center of the novels/films entitled *The Hunger Games*, with the novels/films evolving around that reality show and expanding into a textual universe across media formats. Tom Henthorne makes the point that Collins's novels are produced, circulated, and consumed under digital conditions, which have changed the very nature of textuality. These novels have constructed an immersive, internally-consistent world by combining the familiar with the unfamiliar, intentionally placing gaps in the narrative, and privileging expressiveness over originality, all meant to get readers engaged, inviting them to participate in the meaning-making process and form fan communities (Henthorne 2012: 139–156). As a result, the novels have extended into other formats controlled by media corporations as well as given rise to fan art and activism at the grassroots level. These two extensions correspond to the enchantment controlled by Panem and the dis-/re-enchantment pursued by the protagonists, respectively. *The Hunger Games* is a franchise of transmedia storytelling, the power of which to enchant is intrinsically ambiguous. This section deals with the following questions consecutively: 1) What is transmedia storytelling? 2) How did scholars analyze transmedia practices centered upon Collins's novels? 3) What is the religious/artistic work performed by *The Hunger Games* transmedia assemblage?

6.1 Transmedia Storytelling: An Ever-Expanding Universe

The concept of "transmedia" was first coined by Marsha Kinder and later popularized by Henry Jenkins. Kinder introduced the phrase "transmedia intertextuality" to describe the coalescence of various forms of texts—movies, television series, video games, and toys—into a single commercial system. The example she gave was the program-length commercial targeting young children and training them to move smoothly across different fields of consumption (1991: 41–46). When Jenkins later picked up the term "transmedia," he formulated "transmedia storytelling" to refer to "a new aesthetic that has emerged in response to media convergence—one that places new demands on consumers and depends on the active participation of knowledge communities" (2006: 20–21). That is to say, in the age of media convergence, defined as the co-existence of the old and the new (digital) media, the focus of narratives has shifted from characters and stories to the making of imaginary worlds, a task that cannot be exhausted by a single text, author, or medium.

Transmedia storytelling or transmedia world-building spreads across multiple media platforms such as books, films, television series, games, and a whole range of objects and events related to a franchise, partly official and partly non-licensed, with each text making its own contribution to the whole. The audience actively participates in the making of the imaginary worlds and the production of meaning and sensual experiences. Readers/viewers/players "chase down bits of story across media channels" (Jenkins 2006: 21) and create their own interpretations and spin-offs. Thanks to their enthusiastic engagement, they have moved "from the invisible margins of popular culture and into the center of current thinking about media production and consumption" (Jenkins 2006: 12). As an army of prosumers (consumers doing the work of producers), they are now eagerly courted by media corporations so that their largely unremunerated labor can be absorbed into the cycle of capitalist production, circulation, and consumption.

What Jenkins means by transmedia storytelling consists of *both* the collaborative and creative efforts controlled by media corporations to turn a single product into a series of works across multiple media *and* the reader/viewer/player's exercise of imagination via story-driven explorations into a fictional world to pursue immersive experience. The former is what Derek Johnson calls "media franchising" (2013), or what Stephen Dinehart means by "crossmedia" (quoted in C. Harvey 2014: 278). Dinehart introduces the distinction between "crossmedia" and "transmedia." He uses the former to refer to the licensed expansion of story-worlds aimed at further exploitation, including marketing and merchandising efforts, and reserves the latter for fans' creative work, largely noncommercial. What needs to be taken into account is the interaction of and tension between the big-budget, higher profile variety of transmedia (or, in Dinehart's language, crossmedia) franchises that encompass novels, films, video games, and other commodities on the one hand, and, on the other, micro-budget, Internet (oftentimes social media)-based, and fan-produced projects.

Responding to the need specified above, Colin Harvey proposes that we see the semiotics of transmedia projects as "directly impacted by legal agreements, and by the rules governing intellectual property (IP) rights" (2015: 2). He provides a taxonomy of transmedia practices: the first category identifies the intellectual property in question (such as Collins's novels); the second, directed transmedia storytelling, referring to those transmedia extensions controlled by the IP holder (the films made by Lionsgate that purchased the adaptation right of Collins's novels); the third and the fourth, devolved and detached transmedia storytelling, designating the works deviating from the IP but still controlled by its holder, and those inspired by the IP but without proper license; the fifth, directed transmedia storytelling with user participation describing content produced by consumers of the franchise that is circumscribed by the owners of the IP or the license holders; and the sixth, emergent user-generated transmedia storytelling as represented by the un-licensed fanfiction (Harvey 2014: 282–3).

Harvey's taxonomy covers both the intellectual property owned by media capital and the creative commons of the fans of a particular work. Studying the complicated relationship between contemporary capitalism and transmedia practices, Dan Hassler-Forest further argues that what Michael Hardt and Antonio Negri call Empire is what stands behind intellectual property, while the Multitude backs up creative commons (2016). Empire refers to a world without boundaries and without an outside, one that operates through a new type of sovereignty, which has subsumed the nation-state and extended over social life in its entirety (Hardt and Negri 2000; Brown and Szeman 2002). The Multitude is a new type of political subject (Hardt and Negri 2000) that is "meant to fulfill the function of a mediating social organization between that still-abstract concept (global democracy) and political practice" (Brown and Szeman 2005: 377) by pursuing "singularity plus cooperation, recognition of difference and of the benefit of a common relationship" (Brown and Szeman 2005: 387).

Hassler-Forest highlights the tension within transmedia world-building as located between the corporate-controlled canonical story-worlds that are internally coherent and the radically heterogeneous creative works produced by fan cultures. This internal contradiction, for him, is an expression of *both* the transnational spread of capitalism, which has been commercializing all aspects of life, including the arts, *and* the quest for alternative visions beyond the reigning reality of capitalism and for solidarity beyond gender, race, and class divides.

Despite the tight control exerted by media corporations, the attempts of fans to resist corporate control and break legal parameters help to defer narrative closure and turn a carefully guarded intellectual property into a constantly expanding universe. Acknowledging the liberatory enchantment generated by fans, Hassler-Forest claims that "even as popular story-worlds are constantly being appropriated by capitalism's incontrovertible logic of accumulation, and as audiences' creative work is transformed into immaterial labor at the service of media corporations, there remains a valuable radical potential that is clearly worth salvaging" (2016: 4).

It is to be noted that both Harvey and Hassler-Forest single out science fiction and fantasy, two closely related fantastic genres, as the dominant modes of transmedia world-building. The category of the fantastic emerged simultaneously with literary realism. According to Frederic Jameson, literary realism, a product of demystification and secularization, focused on the embodied individual's realization within the confines of empirical history. By contrast, the fantastic genre, such as science fiction and fantasy, departed from consensus reality to stage ontological plurality beyond the sensorium of the human subject and positivist history. The fantastic was thus an aberrant mode subsumed against and underneath the dominant realist novel and exiled into the realm of mass entertainment, especially children's literature and historical romance—that is, the childish and the bygone.[13] In the current age of media convergence and transmedia world-building, the fantastic genre has gone mainstream and become a new cultural hegemony (Vu 2017). The phenomenal success of *The Hunger Games*, a science fiction text that was written for a young adult audience and has expanded into a transmedia assemblage, is a case in point.

6.2 *Transmedia Practices Extended from Collins's Novels*

Before diving into the relevant scholarship researching how corporate and fan efforts have been building *The Hunger Games* transmedia universe, we need Harvey's six-category taxonomy to map out the terrain. First, Collins's trilogy is the *intellectual property*. Second, Lionsgate's films, the adaptations of the novels, are *directed transmedia storytelling*. Lionsgate, the IP holder, sold licenses to third parties, which developed, produced, and distributed commercial

---

[13] For scholarship on science fiction and fantasy (that is, fantastic novels), see Wolfe 2011; James and Mendlesohn 2003, 2012; Jameson 2013.

products, such as Mattel's Katniss Barbies (Driscoll and Alexandra Heatwole 2018: 4–6) and Subway's bread commercial (Bloomfield 2017: 192). What was practiced in these cases is the third category, *devolved transmedia storytelling*, the products of which are legally safeguarded but do not have to honor the aesthetic and/or political message of the original IP.

Fourth, *detached transmedia storytelling* includes all unauthorized extensions of a transmedia franchise. Represented by fan sites and other fan-produced items, these products, not properly copyrighted, are somehow tolerated by the IP holder because they help to build a fan base and promote the licensed products. The fifth type is *directed transmedia storytelling with user participation*. Examples are the official website for the Lionsgate films, where fans are invited to contribute new content, and the official exhibition that includes a final room showcasing fan arts. Finally, fanfiction and fan activism represent *emergent user-generated transmedia storytelling*. For instance, the Harry Potter Alliance, a nonprofit organized and run by Harry Potter fans, launched a series of campaigns from 2012 to 2015 to protest against real-life inequalities by invoking themes and slogans from *The Hunger Games* novels/films.

Scholars have looked beyond *The Hunger Games* novels/films to consider other types of transmedia storytelling. In this regard, Siobhan McEvoy-Levy (2018) and Catherine Driscoll and Alexandra Heatwole (2018) have investigated the transmedia assemblage evolving beyond Collins's novels and their film adaptations. Examining *The Hunger Games* as a transmedia object "duplicated, elaborated, and repurposed across media, multiplying not only instances but meanings and opportunities for attention" (Driscoll and Heatwole 2018: 3–4), they have considered promotional campaigns, media discourses, commercial products (not always licensed), and fan practices (oftentimes critical of corporate marketing and merchandising). To be more specific, they have looked at Lionsgate's in-house projects such as the official promotional website Captiol.pn and the exhibition on the making of the films; licensed commodities produced by third parties such as a fashion line, cosmetic collection, Katniss Barbie dolls and other toys, and everyday items ranging from school supplies to kitchenwares; and fansites such as the Hunger Games Wiki (http://thehungergames.wikia.com/wiki/The_Hunger_Games_Wiki) and fan productions available at hubs like etsy, redouble, cafepress, or tagged on Pinterest (McEvoy-Levy 2018: 221–264; Driscoll and Heatwole: 2018: 85–98).

The fandom of *The Hunger Games* is a hot topic, with Shannon R. Mortimore-Smith expecting fans to learn to distinguish themselves from the reality TV audience within the novels/films, who are oblivious to the power of their panoptic gaze (2012); Deirdre Anne Evans Garriott studying how teen fans (and adult critics) forwarded particular ideologies by responding to the texts (2014); and Antero Garcia and Marcelle Haddix discussing the racial politics of online fandom (2014). In addition to McEvoy-Levy's work on fanfiction (2018: 265–332) and Nicolle Lamerichs's article on fan fashion (2018), Henry Jenkins (2015), Mélanie Bourdaa (2016), and McEvoy-Levy (2018: 333–372) have studied how fans of *The Hunger Games* protested against the real-life hunger games staged by neoliberal capitalism.

McEvoy-Levy asserts that although *The Hunger Games* novels/films have been dismissed as "children's stories," they grapple with economic inequality, state violence, and the (im)morality of war, terrorism, and revolution. These stories have been deployed in the rhetoric of media commentators and political elites on the one hand, and that of youth activism on the other. She notices that the novels/films have been used to "justify ideologies from both the left and right of the political spectrum" and that the allegedly politically inert young people, through writing/reading fanfiction and participating in fan activism, have turned YA literature into a platform on which they articulate their own concerns and pursue social engagement (McEvoy-Levy 2018: 4). Likewise, Driscoll and Heatwole point out that fandom, the quest for textual immersion and shared passion, has been particularly associated with not just children but also women. Both women and children are portrayed as obsessed individuals that form a hysterical crowd; however, what they have created is a creative commons against the endless extraction of capitalism (2018: 90). They have also been struggling to build alternative worlds beyond the all-encompassing Empire. However, David Baker and Elena Schak caution us against an overly optimistic celebration of fan power. They remind us that despite the feminist potentials of *The Hunger Games* original novels, the transmedia world, undeniably dominated by commercial imperatives, offers limited opportunities for change in terms of gender and other issues (2019).

6.3 *The Work of Religion/Art and* The Hunger Games *Transmedia Assemblage*

The previous sections demonstrated that the seemingly religion-less diegetic space of *The Hunger Games* novels/films turns out to be teeming with religion, as long as we reconsider the very category of religion. Religion is not defined by interiorized piety in some transcendent existence, not limited to established institutions and communities, and/or not separated from state politics at the top and everyday life at the bottom. We also need to reconsider the very idea of art in the age of transmedia storytelling, starting with the work of art defined as a fluid process rather than a fixed product, since the novels have extended into the films and an entire array of corporate and fan projects. The search for religion, both established traditions and emerging iterations, has new territories to cover. Likewise, the making of art has broken new ground.

Beyond the boundaries of the novels/films, religion—or, more specifically, Christianity—has intruded into the devolved, detached, and emergent user-generated types of transmedia storytelling. With regard to licensed extensions, one example is the abundance of Christian imagery in the soundtracks of the films (Swanson 2016). If we shift our attention from corporate marketing and merchandising to fan reception, how Christian communities responded to the novels, films, and related products is a question to be addressed. So far, no research has been done on religion and *The Hunger Games* fandom. Andrew Crome's work on the Christian fanworks devoted to the *My Little Pony* franchise (2014, 2015) may serve as a model. Christian communities and *The Hunger Games* fan communities do overlap, although some Christians were highly critical of the franchise. A quick Internet search would take us to numerous sites and forums where *The Hunger Games* novels/films were heatedly discussed by Christians. At Amazon, books that discuss the parallels between *The Hunger Games* novels/films and the Gospel are available, such as Julie Clawson's *The Hunger Games and the Gospel: Bread, Circuses, and the Kingdom of God* (2012) and Andy Lanford and Ann Duncun's *The Gospel According to* The Hunger Games *Trilogy* (2012).

What parallel these popular commentaries that bring together the trilogy and the Christian tradition are scholarly writings that perform the same task, such as McAvan's (2017) and Williams's (2017) discussion of sacrifice and the making of the sacred, Bloomfield's assertion of bread as a symbol of sacrifice and thanksgiving (2017), and articles by McDonald (2012, 2014) and Gant (2012) that view art as a form of soul-shaping spirituality. Working along the same line, Karl Hand pairs the low-brow young adult fiction with the Lukan pulp fiction—that is, Luke's "reversal of method" periscope (Luke 22:35–38). Hand points out that in the face of imperial oppression, "Jesus releases his disciples from their call to the radical itinerant mission of Luke 10:1–12" (2015: 349), and instead gives them the new instructions to take up a dagger. What *The Hunger Games* series helps to invoke is what Luke preserved for us: "a memory of Jesus who himself knew and taught conversion to revolutionary consciousness" (Hand 2015: 349). Following Hand's lead, Darren Cronshaw reads *The Hunger Games* as a work of public theology, a story that addresses issues of Empire and strives to balance personal sovereignty and self-fulfillment with the struggle for social and political changes (2019).

Fanfiction that adds religion into the original story-world is another uncharted ground awaiting scholarly exploration. Searching tags such as "religion," "the spiritual," and "the supernatural," I browsed *The Hunger Games* fanfiction at fanfiction.net and archiveofourown.org. In my observation, religion has made its inroads into fanfiction writings via at least three routes: filling-the-gaps, crossovers, and alternate universes.

First, in stories that add new details to the original setting of the canon (source text on which fanfiction is based), some fans were curious about the secularity of Panem and chose to invent the "hidden" religious traditions of Panem. To give a few examples: "Carols of the Districts" depicts how Christmas is celebrated in each district (https://archiveofourown.org/works/5392949); "The Passover" portrays Beetee and Wiress, two minor characters from District 3, as Jews and focuses on how they retell the story of Moses (https://archiveofourown.org/works/5392949); and in "Deep in the Meadow," the author writes about Rue's encounter with Jesus in her afterlife (https://www.fanfiction.net/s/10552662/1/Deep-in-the-Meadow).

The second type consists of crossovers that combine *The Hunger Games* story-world with other popular franchises such as the *Percy Jackson* series, the television show *The Supernatural*, and Marvel comics/films, which have reinvented world mythologies. There are also stories that combine *The Hunger Games* with literary canons such as the *Iliad* and the *Divine Comedy*. For instance, in "Without Dionysius," Dionysius is portrayed as a TV host interviewing the tributes and their families (https://archiveofourown.org/works/2210985). "The Hunger Games" is a short story in which Virgil and Dante become tributes in the Hunger Games (https://archiveofourown.org/works/4276560).

Last but not the least, there are alternate universe stories that change the setting and/or other narrative elements of the source text. Fanfic writers interested in religion have transported their favorite characters to Medieval France, colonial America, or the contemporary world. In "Inquisitio," Katniss and her friends are interrogated by Brother Coriolanus Snow of the Order of Preachers for being Waldensians, heretics who practiced poverty and helped the poor (https://archiveofourown.org/works/529705). In "Dark Fire," Katniss is a girl fighting against witch-hunting in New England (https://www.fanfiction.net/s/8527951/1/Darkfire). There are also a few stories that enact Peeta as either a seminarian or a pastor struggling with his sexual attraction to Katniss, such as "Practice Run" (https://archiveofourown.org/works/11038224/chapters/24603885), "Sins and Redemption" (https://archiveofourown.org/works/8602516?view_adult=true), and "Not So Chaste" (https://archiveofourown.org/works/749986/chapters/1399593).

It is no exaggeration to say that religion is highly visible in fanfiction. Why are these fanfiction writers interested in religion? What are their presumptions of religion? What are the real-life issues they have endeavored to engage by writing religion into the transmedia universe of *The Hunger Games*? What are the contributions they have made to the always on-going discursive (trans)-formation of religion? These are some of the questions that future researchers may want to wrestle with.

While pre-existing religious traditions have found their way into the ever-expanding textual universe of *The Hunger Games*, this transmedia assemblage as a whole has been doing the type of religious/artistic work conceptualized by Jackson, Morgan, and Chidester. Yonah Ringlestein (2013) argues that transmedia storytelling as exemplified by *The Hunger Games* universe is what Chidester calls the "authentic fake" (2005)—a nonreligious entity doing real religious work. I add that this type of religious work is what Jackson means by the convergence of religion and art and what Morgan refers to as enchantment.

Ringlestein compares transmedia franchises with religious traditions. Both invent rituals and narratives and invite consumers/followers to seek a sense of order, unity, and belonging in a fragmented world. In short, both engage in world-building. Established religions encompass transmedia elements. For instance, traditions such as Christian Gnosticism and Jewish Kabbalism provided material and symbolic fragments scattered across multiple media platforms to their devotees, who were charged with a personal responsibility to practice negotiation and reintegration to achieve a sense of wholeness, or, in Chidester's language, to transpose incongruity into moments of congruence. Similarly, contemporary transmedia franchises, according to Ringlestein, do religious/artistic work because they construct imaginary worlds and enable consumers to fulfill their desire for unity.

Ringlestein studies the enthusiasm of *The Hunger Games* fans to grasp the entire story-world and participate in the meaning-making process. Raising the question of why young fans are eager to inhabit the inhospitable dystopian world of Panem, he explains that they have made an attempt to quench the hunger for reality and completeness in a world of fragmented information. They not just quest for individual wholeness but also strive to build communities. They identify with Katniss, "confused and surrounded by manipulated and multiplying realities, seeking to bring all the disparate elements in her life back into a unified whole" (Ringlestein 2013: 384), taking her as a role model and learning from her to take a critical perspective when negotiating with various media to seek reunification.

It is unfortunate that Ringlestein limits his attention to the novels/films rather than investigating fan works and activities that not only expand but also alter the original franchise. Although highly inspiring, his argument has at least two weak points. First, he expects the fans to learn to differentiate between artifice and reality—that is, to apply the critical reflexivity they learn from Katniss to all constructed worlds and realities, whether "the singular reality of modernity ... [or] the plural, fluid, malleable realities of postmodernity" (2013: 384). However, I wonder why and how this distinction would be productive in the age of the real-hyperreal and human-nonhuman fusions. Second, Ringlestein overlooks the tension between corporate-controlled and fan-produced projects, a point Hassler-Forest stresses in his reading of *The Hunger Games* transmedia universe. Instead of differentiating between artifice and reality, we need to find out what kind of religious/artistic work is done by this transmediated religion. Does it serve the enchantment of media corporations and the Empire of global capitalism or channel the dis-/re-enchantment of grassroots creativity from which Multitude is to rise? Do we—readers, viewers, fans, critics, and scholars outside the fictional world—side with the Capitol of Panem or Katniss and Peeta, the rebellious tributes?

Hassler-Forest's discussion of the transmedia projects of *The Hunger Games* is illuminating when we turn to examine the split enchantment performed by Ringlestein's transmediated religion. Hassler-Forest's central thesis is that the transmedia world-building performed by the big corporations articulates the cultural and political logic of Empire by offering immersive, complex, and endlessly expanding narrative environments in which audiences can safely negotiate the tensions and contradictions of capitalism. Seen differently, the creative work of fan participation is a form of immaterial (or, more precisely, affective) labor that operates both in collaboration with and in opposition to new forms of corporate power. In this regard, he reconciles Jenkins (2006, 2015) and Christian Fuchs (2017), the former valorizing fan work as a form of protest and resistance while the latter argues that the digital labor performed by fans is exploited by media capital. Not always at the service of media corporations and capitalist accumulation, the creative work of fans is a site where existing imaginary worlds are transformed, alternative possibilities are postulated, and collaborative communities keep emerging and expanding. It is a site for the emergence of Multitude.

Transmedia world-building is infused with power: the power of Empire to enchant us—to commodify everything and turn us into competitive individuals fighting our daily hunger games—and the dis-/re-enchanting power of Multitude, which claims that another world is possible. These two powers compete with each other and are entangled in transmedia universes such as *The Hunger Games*. Hassler-Forest examines this entanglement at three levels: in the organization of story-world, in the narrative itself, and in the creative work done by a participating audience. Under his influence, at these three levels I conclude my critical appraisal of *The Hunger Games* scholarship.

First, the story-world of the novels/films is divided into the rich Capitol and the exploited Districts, corresponding to the class divide and conflicts of our lived reality. I have analyzed this story-world in the previous sections. It is centered upon the state ritual of the Hunger Games, a Hobbesian war of everyone against everyone that makes Panem sacred, where the reigning ideology is a creepy hybridization of authoritarian statism and neoliberal individualism (section 2). What is counterposed with the Hunger Games is the religious/artistic practices of the protagonists, such as Katniss's singing, Peeta's painting, and the material network of the mockingjay (section 3). In this story-world, the repressive enchantment of the Hunger Games and the liberatory enchantment of religious/artistic tactics intertwine within and beyond the game arenas and TV screens. Media industry, or, more specifically, reality TV, a church-like institution, plays a central role in consolidating the Capitol's political and economic power. However, the participants and audiences of the reality show know how to twist the discourse of the real to their own advantage (section 4). On a larger scale, everyday life represented by material objects such as food and clothing and embodied practices of eating and dressing is also both regulated by the state and open to the re-appropriation and resignification of the ordinary people (section 5).

The narrative (plotline) of *The Hunger Games* novels/films, in the reading of Hassler-Forest, is deeply ambiguous. Driven by an anti-capitalist sentiment, the narrative ends on a note of disillusionment in revolution, with Katniss breaking away from the rebellious District 13 and retreating into family life. Hassler-Forest sees this ambiguity as having contributed to the phenomenal success of the franchise, as readers on the right and the left have all recognized their concerns in it. Scholars have also produced contradictory readings. Hand (2015) and Aitchison (2015), among many others, highlight the theme of revolution in the novels/films in association with the Gospel of Luke and the modern rewritings of Spartacus, respectively. However, Trites views the ideological position of Collins "as very close to Libertarianism—the underlying ethics of which involves an inherent distrust of any government" (2014: 26). Similarly, Andrew Tate questions whether the novels, among many other YA dystopias, tell a conformist tale disguised as subversive (2017: 103–128). In this regard, Ben Murnane's investigation into the right-wing appropriation of Collins as the new Ayn Rand is particularly interesting (2018). Clearly the conflicting versions of enchantment are in place.

At the level of the audience's participation in making *The Hunger Games* transmedia universe, both left-wing and right-wing ideologies can be identified. McEvoy-Levy reports that "[i]n the United States, the Tea Party Patriots produced a Hunger Games-based political film critiquing the Obama administration's policies and held a Capitol games party (with Hunger Games costumes encouraged). Progressive Governor Elizabeth Warren was depicted as Katniss at one of her campaign events and was photographed giving District 12's three-fingered salute. Donald Trump's daughter Ivanka tweeted a picture of herself "'channeling her inner Katniss' at an archery range" (2018: 4). Enchantment never ceases to be a field of contestations.

Away from the world of political elites, the ordinary fans may want to consider the question Hassler-Forest raises: Are you to work as prosumers to valorize media capital or to protest against inequality and injustice, following the lead of The Harry Potter Association's campaign "Odds in Our Favor" (2016: 145–147)? This is also the question we may want to direct at the work of religion/art, whether transmediated or not. What exactly is the work of religion/art? To serve the enchantment of ideological values and media-industrial practices that reinforce Empire, or to channel the non-/anti-capitalist energy of Multitude into the alternative enchantment of a future beyond the dominant symbolic and material order? With these questions, I conclude this survey.

Bibliography

Primary Texts

Collins, Susan. 2008. *The Hunger Games*. New York: Scholastic Inc.
Collins, Susan. 2009. *Catching Fire*. New York: Scholastic Inc.
Collins, Susan. 2010. *Mockingjay*. New York: Scholastic Inc.
The Hunger Games. 2012. Directed by Gary Ross. USA: Lionsgate.
The Hunger Games: Catching Fire. 2013. Directed by Francis Lawrence. USA: Lionsgate.
The Hunger Games: Mockingjay—Part 1. 2014. Directed by Francis Lawrence. USA: Lionsgate.
The Hunger Games: Mockingjay—Part 2. 2015. Directed by Francis Lawrence. USA: Lionsgate.

Secondary Scholarship

Agamben, Giorgio. 1998. *Homo Sacer: Sovereign Power and Bare Life*. Translated by Daniel Heller-Roazen. Stanford, CA: Stanford University Press.
Agamben, Giorgio. 2000. *Means Without End: Notes on Politics*. Translated by Vincenzo Binetti and Cesare Casarino.
Minneapolis: University of Minnesota Press.
Aitchison, David. 2015. "*The Hunger Games*, Spartacus, and Other Family Stories: Sentimental Revolution in Contemporary Young-Adult Fiction." *The Lion and the Unicorn* Vol. 39, No. 3: 254–274.

Albala, Ken, ed. 2019. *Routledge International Handbook of Food Studies*. Routledge.
Andrejevic, Mark. 2004. *Reality TV: The Work of Being Watched*. Lanham, MD: Rowman & Littlefield Publishers.
Apostolos-Cappadona, Diane. 2017. *Religion and the Arts: History and Method*. Leiden: Brill.
Asad, Talal. 2001. "Reading a Modern Classic: W. C. Smith's 'The Meaning and End of Religion.'" In Hent de Vries and Samuel Weber, eds., *Religion and Media*. Stanford, CA: Stanford University Press, pp. 131–147.
Asad, Talal. 2009. *Genealogies of Religion: Discipline and Reasons of Power in Christianity and Islam*. Baltimore, MD: Johns Hopkins University Press.
Baker, Carissa Ann. 2014. "Outside the Seam: The Construction of and Relationship to Panem's Nature." In Deirdre Anne Evans Garriott, Whitney Elaine Jones, and Julie Elizabeth Tyler, eds., *Space and Place in* The Hunger Games*: New Readings of the Novels*. Jefferson, NC: McFarland, pp. 198–219.
Baker, David, and Elena Schak. 2019. "*The Hunger Games*: Transmedia, Gender and Possibility." *Continuum: Journal of Media & Cultural Studies* Vol. 33, No. 2: 201–215.
Barthes, Roland. 1983. *The Fashion System*. Translated by Matthew Ward and Richard Howard. New York: Hill and Wang.
Barthes, Roland. 1997. "Toward a Psychosociology of Contemporary Food Consumption." In Carole Counihan, Penny Van Esterik, and Alice P. Julier, eds., *Food and Culture: A Reader*. New York: Routledge, pp. 20–27.
Bataille, Georges. 1988. *The Accursed Share: An Essay on General Economy*. Translated by Robert Hurley. New York: Zone Books.
Baudrillard, Jean. 1998. *The Consumer Society: Myths and Structures*. Translated by Turner Chris. London; Thousand Oaks, CA: Sage.
Baudrillard, Jean. 2017. *Symbolic Exchange and Death*. Translated by Iain Hamilton Grant. Revised edition. London: Sage.
Baudrillard, Jean. 1994. *Simulacra and Simulation*. Translated by Sheila Glaser. Ann Arbor: University of Michigan Press.
Baudrillard, Jean. 2005. "Violence of the Virtual and Integral Reality." *International Journal of Baudrillard Studies* Vol. 2, No. 2: 1–16.
Baudrillard, Jean. 2011. *Telemorphosis: Preceded by Dust Breeding*. Translated by Drew Burk. Minneapolis, MN: Univocal.
Benjamin, Walter, et al. 2008. *The Work of Art in the Age of Its Technological Reproducibility, and Other Writings on Media*. Translated by Edmund Jephcott. Cambridge, MA: Belknap Press of Harvard University Press.
Blasingame, James, and Suzanne Collins. 2009. "An Interview with Suzanne Collins." *Journal of Adolescent & Adult Literacy* Vol. 52, No. 8 (May): 726–727.
Bloomfield, Jem. 2017. "'My Eucharist to the People of District 11': Bread, Sacrifice and Thanksgiving in *The Hunger Games*." *Theology* Vol. 120, No. 3: 190–196.

Bourdaa, Mélanie. 2016. "'I Am not a Tribute': The Transmedia Strategy of *The Hunger Games* versus Fan Activism." In Benjamin W. L. Derhy Kurtz and Mélanie Bourdaa, eds., *The Rise of Transtexts: Challenges and Opportunities*. New York: Routledge, pp. 104–117.

Bourdieu, Pierre, and Randal Johnson. 1993. *The Field of Cultural Production: Essays on Art and Literature*. New York: Columbia University Press.

Bourdieu, Pierre. 1990. *The Logic of Practice*. Translated by Richard Nice. Stanford. CA: Stanford University Press.

Bourdieu, Pierre. 2000. *Distinction: A Social Critique of the Judgement of Taste*. Translated by Richard Nice. Cambridge, MA: Harvard University Press.

Bourdon, Jérôme. 2008. "Self-Despotism: Reality Television and the New Subject of Politics." *Framework: The Journal of Cinema and Media* Vol. 49, No. 1: 66–82.

Boyce, Charlotte, and Joan Fitzpatrick. 2017. *A History of Food in Literature: From the Fourteenth Century to the Present*. Abingdon, Oxon; New York: Routledge.

Britt, Brian. 2012. "Secularism and the Question of the 'Judeo-Christian.'" *Relegere: Studies in Religion and Reception* Vol. 2, No. 2: 343–52.

Broad, Katherine R. 2013. "'The Dandelion in the Spring': Utopia as Romance in Suzanne Collins's *The Hunger Games* Trilogy." In Balaka Basu, Katherine R. Broad, and Carrie Hintz, eds., *Contemporary Dystopian Fiction for Young Adults: Brave New Teenagers*. New York: Routledge, pp. 117–130.

Brown, Frank Burch, ed. 2013. *The Oxford Handbook of Religion and the Arts*. New York: Oxford University Press.

Brown, Nicholas, and Imre Szeman. 2002. "The Global Coliseum: On Empire." *Cultural Studies* Vol. 16, No. 2: 177–192.

Brown, Nicholas, and Imre Szeman. 2005. "What Is the Multitude? Questions for Michael Hardt and Antonio Negri." *Cultural Studies* Vol. 19, No. 3: 372–387.

Bryne, Deirdre. 2015. "Dressed for the Part: An Analysis of Clothing in Suzanne Collins's *Hunger Games* Trilogy." *Journal of Literary Studies* Vol. 31, No. 2: 43–62.

Carrette, Jeremy R. 1999. "Prologue to a Confession of the Flesh." In Michel Foucault and Jeremy R. Carrette, *Religion and Culture*. New York: Routledge, pp. 1–47.

Cettl, Fani. 2015. "Revisiting Dystopia: The Reality Show Biopolitics of 'The Hunger Games.'" *Культура/Culture* Vol. 5. No. 12: 139–145.

Chidester, David. 2005. *Authentic Fakes: Religion and American Popular Culture*. Berkeley: University of California Press.

Chidester, David. 2018. *Religion: Material Dynamics*. Oakland, California: University of California Press.

Clack, Beverley. 1999. *Misogyny in the Western Philosophical Tradition: A Reader*. New York: Routledge.

Clemente, Bill. 2012. "Panem in America: Crisis Economics and a Call for Political Engagement." In Mary F. Pharr and Leisa A. Clark, eds., *Of Bread, Blood and* The

Hunger Games: *Critical Essays on the Suzanne Collins Trilogy*. Jefferson, NC: McFarland, pp. 20–29.

Cone, James H. 1972. *The Spirituals and the Blues: An Interpretation*. New York: Seabury Press.

Cone, James H. 2011. *The Cross and the Lynching Tree*. Maryknoll, New York: Orbis Books.

Connors, Sean P. 2014a. "I Try to Remember Who I Am and Who I Am Not: The Subjugation of Nature and Women in *The Hunger Games*." In Sean P. Connors, ed., *The Politics of Panem: Challenging Genres*. Rotterdam: Sense Publishers, pp. 137–156.

Connors, Sean P. 2014b. "I Was Watching You, Mockingjay: Surveillance, Tactics, and the Limits of Panopticism." In Sean P. Connors, ed., *The Politics of Panem: Challenging Genres*. Rotterdam: Sense Publishers, pp. 85–102.

Couldry, Nick. 2009. "Teaching Us to Fake It: The Ritualized Norms of Television's Reality Games." In Susan Murray and Laurie Ouellette, eds., *Reality TV: Remaking Television Culture. 2nd Ed.* New York: New York University Press, pp. 57–74.

Counihan, Carole, Penny Van Esterik, and Alice P. Julier, eds. 1997. *Food and Culture: A Reader*. New York: Routledge.

Craik, Jennifer. 1994. *The Face of Fashion: Cultural Studies in Fashion*. London; New York: Routledge.

Crome, Andrew. 2014. "Reconsidering Religion and Fandom: Christian Fan Works in *My Little Pony* Fandom." *Culture and Religion* Vol. 15, No. 4: 399–418.

Crome, Andrew. 2015. "Religion and the Pathologization of Fandom: Religion, Reason, and Controversy in *My Little Pony* Fandom." *The Journal of Religion and Popular Culture* Vol. 27, No. 2: 130–147.

Cronshaw, Darren. 2019. "Resisting the Empire in Young Adult Fiction: Lessons from Hunger Games." *International Journal of Public Theology* Vol. 13, No. 2: 119–139.

Day, Helen. 2012. "Simulacra, Sacrifice and Survival in *The Hunger Games*, *Battle Royale*, and *The Running Man*." In Mary F. Pharr and Leisa A. Clark, eds., *Of Bread, Blood and* The Hunger Games: *Critical Essays on the Suzanne Collins Trilogy*. Jefferson, NC: McFarland, pp. 167–178.

de Certeau, Michel, et al. 1998. *The Practice of Everyday Life, Vol. 2, Living and Cooking*. Translated by Timothy J. Tomaski. Minneapolis: University of Minnesota Press.

de Certeau, Michel. 1984. *The Practice of Everyday Life*. Translated by Steven F. Rendall. Berkeley: University of California Press.

De Vries, Hent. 2001. "In Media Res: Global Religion, Public Spheres, and the Task of Contemporary Comparative Religious Studies." In Hent de Vries and Samuel Weber, eds., *Religion and Media*. Stanford, CA: Stanford University Press, pp. 3–32.

Debord, Guy. 1994. *The Society of the Spectacle*. Translated by Donald Nicholson-Smith. New York: Zone Books.

Debord, Guy. 1998. *Comments on the Society of the Spectacle*. Translated by Malcolm Imrie. London; New York: Verso.

Derrida, Jacques. 1992. *Given Time: I. Counterfeit Money*. Translated by Peggy Kamuf. Chicago: University of Chicago Press.

Derrida, Jacques. 1995. *The Gift of Death*. Translated by David Wills. Chicago: University of Chicago Press.

Despain, Max. 2012. "The 'Fine Reality of Hunger Satisfied': Food as Cultural Metaphor in Panem." In Mary F. Pharr and Leisa A. Clark, eds., *Of Bread, Blood and* The Hunger Games: *Critical Essays on the Suzanne Collins Trilogy*. Jefferson, NC: McFarland, pp. 69–79.

Driscoll, Catherine, and Alexandra Heatwole. 2018. *The Hunger Games: Spectacle, Risk and the Girl Action Hero*. London: Routledge, Taylor & Francis Group.

Dubrofsky, Rachel E., and Emily D. Ryalls. 2014. "The Hunger Games: Performing Not-performing to Authenticate Femininity and Whiteness." *Critical Studies in Media Communication* Vol. 31, No. 5: 395–409.

Durkheim, Émile. 1995. *The Elementary Forms of Religious Life*. Translated and with an introduction by Karen E. Fields. New York: Free Press.

Eberl, Jason T. 2012. "'No Mutt is Good'—Really?: Creating Interspecies Chimeras." In William Irwin, ed., The Hunger Games *and Philosophy: A Critique of Pure Treason*. Hoboken, NJ: John Wiley & Sons, pp. 121–132.

Eicher, Joanne B., and Lynne Hume. 2013. *The Religious Life of Dress: Global Fashion and Faith*. London: Bloomsbury Publishing.

Einstein, Mara, Katherine Madden, and Diane Winston, eds. 2018. *Religion and Reality TV: Faith in Late Capitalism*. Abingdon, Oxon; New York: Routledge.

Entwistle, Joanne. 2000. *The Fashioned Body: Fashion, Dress and Modern Social Theory*. Cambridge: Polity Press; Malden, MA: Blackwell.

Epstein, Heidi. 2004. *Melting the Venusberg: A Feminist Theology of Music*. New York: Continuum.

Farnell, Lorna, and Donna Lee Brien. 2018. *The Routledge Companion to Literature and Food*. New York: Routledge.

Fessenden, Tracy. 2018. *Religion Around Billie Holiday*. University Park, PA: Pennsylvania State University Press.

Fisher, Mark. 2012. "Precarious Dystopias: *The Hunger Games*, *In Time*, and *Never Let Me Go*." *Film Quarterly* Vol. 65, No. 4: 27–33.

Fitzgerald, Jon, and Philip Hayward. 2015. "Mountain Airs, Mockingjays and Modernity: Songs and Their Significance in *The Hunger Games*." *Science Fiction Film & Television* Vol. 8, No. 1: 75–89.

Foucault, Michel. 1982. "The Subject and Power." *Critical Inquiry* Vol. 8, No. 4: 777–795.

Foucault, Michel. 1995. *Discipline and Punish: The Birth of the Prison*. Translated by Alan Sheridan. New York: Vintage Books.

Foucault, Michel. 1997. "Security, Territory, and Population." In Paul Rabinow, ed., *Ethics: Subjectivity and Truth (The Essential Works of Foucault, 1954–1984, Vol. 1)*. Translated by Robert Hurley and others. New York: New Press, pp. 67–71.

Foucault, Michel. 1999. "Pastoral Power and Political Reason." In Jeremy R. Carrette, ed., *Religion and Culture*. New York: Routledge, pp. 135–152.

Fuchs, Christian. 2014. *Social Media: A Critical Introduction*. London: Sage.

Ganger, John. 2010a. "Mockingjay Discussion 15: The Hanging Tree." (August 25). *Hogwartsprofessor.com*. URL: https://www.hogwartsprofessor.com/mockingjay-discussion-15-the-hanging-tree/.

Ganger, John. 2010b. "Mockingjay Discussion 16: Katniss' Meadow Song." (August 26). *Hogwartsprofessor.com*. URL: https://www.hogwartsprofessor.com/mockingjay-discussion-16-katniss-meadow-song/.

Gant, Tammy L. 2012. "Hungering for Righteousness: Music, Spirituality and Katniss Everdeen." In Mary F. Pharr and Leisa A. Clark, eds., *Of Bread, Blood and* The Hunger Games: *Critical Essays on the Suzanne Collins Trilogy*. Jefferson, NC: McFarland, pp. 89–97.

Garcia, Antero, and Marcelle Haddix. 2014. "The Revolution Starts with Rue: Online Fandom and The Racial Politics of the Hunger Games." In Sean P. Connors, ed., *The Politics of Panem: Challenging Genres*. Rotterdam: Sense Publishers, pp. 203–217.

Garriott, Deirdre Anne Evans. 2014. "Performing the Capitol in Digital Spaces: The Punitive Gaze of the Panopticon among Fans and Critics." In Deirdre Anne Evans Garriott, Whitney Elaine Jones, and Julie Elizabeth Tyler, eds., *Space and Place in* The Hunger Games: *New Readings of the Novels*. Jefferson, NC: McFarland, pp. 160–183.

Geertz, Clifford. 1973. *The Interpretation of Cultures*. New York: Basic Books.

Gilbert-Hickey, Meghan. 2016. "Gender Rolls: Bread and Resistance in the 'Hunger Games' Trilogy." In Claudia Nelson, Miranda A. Green-Barteet, and Amy L. Montz, eds., *Female Rebellion in Young Adult Dystopian Fiction*. Farnham, Surrey, UK; Burlington, VT: Ashgate, pp. 95–106.

Girard, René. 1977. *Violence and the Sacred*. Translated by Patrick Gregory. Baltimore: Johns Hopkins University Press.

Girard, René. 1986. *The Scapegoat*. Translated by Yvonne Freccero. Baltimore: Johns Hopkins University Press.

Gray, Jonathan. 2009. "Cinderella Burps: Gender, Performativity, and the Dating Show." In Susan Murray and Laurie Ouellette, eds., *Reality TV: Remaking Television Culture*. 2nd Ed. New York: New York University Press, pp. 260–277.

Guanio-Uluru, Lykke. 2017. "Katniss Everdeen's Posthuman Identity in Suzanne Collins's *Hunger Games* Series: Free as a Mockingjay?" *Jeunesse: Young People, Texts, Cultures* Vol. 9, No. 1: 57–81.

Hand, Karl. 2015. "Come Now, Let Us Treason Together: Conversion and Revolutionary Consciousness in Luke 23:35–38 and *The Hunger Games* Trilogy." *Literature and Theology* Vol. 29, No. 3: 348–65.

Hanlon, Tina L. 2012. "Coal Dust and Ballads: Appalachia and District 12." In Mary F. Pharr and Leisa A. Clark, eds., *Of Bread, Blood and* The Hunger Games*: Critical Essays on the Suzanne Collins Trilogy*. Jefferson, NC: McFarland, pp. 59–68.

Hansen, Kathryn Strong. 2015. "The Metamorphosis of Katniss Everdeen: *The Hunger Games*, Myth, and Femininity." *Children's Literature Association Quarterly* Vol. 40, No. 2: 161–178.

Hardt, Michael, and Antonio Negri. 2000. *Empire*. Cambridge, MA: Harvard University Press.

Hardt, Michael, and Antonio Negri. 2004. *Multitude: War and Democracy in the Age of Empire*. New York: Penguin Press.

Harvey, Colin B. 2014. "A Taxonomy of Transmedia Storytelling." In Marie-Laure Ryan and Jan-Noël Thon, eds., *Storyworlds Across Media: Toward a Media-conscious Narratology*. Lincoln: University of Nebraska Press, pp. 278–294.

Harvey, Colin B. 2015. *Fantastic Transmedia: Narrative, Play and Memory Across Science Fiction and Fantasy Storyworlds*. London: Palgrave Macmillan.

Harvey, Graham. 2013. *Food, Sex and Strangers: Understanding Religion as Everyday Life*. Durham: Acumen Pub.

Hassler-Forest, Dan. 2016. *Science Fiction, Fantasy, and Politics: Transmedia Worldbuilding beyond Capitalism*. London; New York: Rowman & Littlefield International.

Hazard, Sonia. 2013. "The Material Turn in the Study of Religion." *Religion and Society* Vol. 4, No. 1: 58–78.

Heit, Jamey. 2015. *The Politics of* The Hunger Games. Jefferson, NC: McFarland.

Henthorne, Tom. 2012. *Approaching the Hunger Games Trilogy: A Literary and Cultural Analysis*. Jefferson, NC: McFarland.

Hill, Annette. 2014. *Reality TV*. London; New York: Routledge.

Hirschkind, Charles. 2011. "Media, Mediation, Religion." *Social Anthropology/Anthropologie Sociale* Vol. 19, No. 1: 90–97.

Hobbes, Thomas, G. A. J. Rogers, and Karl Schuhmann. 2005. *Thomas Hobbes: Leviathan. A Critical Edition*. London: Continuum.

Horkheimer, Max, and Theodor W. Adorno. 1993. *Dialectic of Enlightenment*. Translated by John Cumming. New York: Continuum.

Hubert, Henri, Marcel Mauss, and E. E. Evans-Pritchard. 1981. *Sacrifice: Its Nature and Functions*. Translated by W. D. Halls. Chicago: University of Chicago Press.

Hubler, Angela E. 2014. "Utopia and Anti-Utopia in Lois Lowry's and Suzanne Collins's Dystopian Fiction." In Angela E. Hubler, ed., *Little Red Readings: Historical Materialist Perspectives on Children's Literature*. Jackson: University Press of Mississippi, pp. 228–244.

Hudson, Hannah Trierweiler. 2010. "Sit Down with Suzanne Collins." *Instructor* Vol. 120, No. 2: 51–53.

Jackson, Michael. 2016. *The Work of Art: Rethinking the Elementary Forms of Religious Life*. New York: Columbia University Press.

James, Edward, and Farah Mendlesohn, eds. 2003. *The Cambridge Companion to Science Fiction*. Cambridge, UK; New York: Cambridge University Press.

James, Edward, and Farah Mendlesohn, eds. 2012. *The Cambridge Companion to Fantasy Literature*. Cambridge, UK; New York: Cambridge University Press.

Jameson, Fredric. 2013. *The Antinomies of Realism*. London: Verso.

Jenkins, Henry. 2006. *Convergence Culture: Where Old and New Media Collide*. New York: New York University Press.

Jenkins, Henry. 2015. "'Cultural Acupuncture': Fan Activism and the Harry Potter Alliance." In Lincoln Geraghty, ed., *Popular Media Cultures: Fans, Audiences, and Paratexts*. London: Palgrave MacMillan, pp. 206–229.

Jobling, Paul. 2015. "Roland Barthes: Semiology and the Rhetorical Codes of Fashion." In Agnès Rocamora and Anneke Smelik, eds., *Thinking Through Fashion: A Guide to Key Theorists*. London: I. B. Tauris, pp. 132–148.

Johnson, Derek. 2013. *Media Franchising: Creative License and Collaboration in the Culture Industries*. New York: New York University Press.

Kellner, Douglas. 2003. *Media Spectacle*. London; New York: Routledge.

Kinder, Marsha. 1991. *Playing with Power in Movies, Television, and Video Games: From Muppet Babies to Teenage Mutant Ninja Turtles*. Berkeley: University of California Press.

King, Sharon D. 2012. "(Im)Mutable Natures: Animal, Human and Hybrid Horror." In Mary F. Pharr and Leisa A. Clark, eds., *Of Bread, Blood and* The Hunger Games: *Critical Essays on the Suzanne Collins Trilogy*. Jefferson, NC: McFarland, pp. 108–17.

Koenig, Gretchen. "Communal Spectacle: Reshaping History and Memory through Violence." In Mary F. Pharr and Leisa A. Clark, eds., *Of Bread, Blood and* The Hunger Games: *Critical Essays on the Suzanne Collins Trilogy*. Jefferson, NC: McFarland, pp. 39–48.

Krikowa, Natalie. 2018. "Experiencing the Cityscapes and Rural Landscapes as 'Citizens' of *The Hunger Games* Storyworld." In Yael Maurer and Meyrav Koren-Kuik, eds., *Cityscapes of the Future: Urban Spaces in Science Fiction*. Leiden: Brill-Rodopi, pp. 151–167.

Lamerichs, Nicolle. 2018. "Fan Fashion: Re-enacting Hunger Games Through Clothing and Design." In Paul Booth, ed., *A Companion to Media Fandom and Fan Studies*. Hoboken, NJ: Wiley Blackwell, pp. 175–188.

Latham, Don, and Jonathan M. Hollister. 2014. "The Games People Play: Information and Media Literacies in *The Hunger Games* Trilogy." *Children's Literature in Education* Vol. 45, No. 1: 33–46.

Lem, Ellyn, and Holly Hassel. 2012. "'Killer' Katniss and 'Lover Boy' Peeta: Suzanne Collins's Defiance of Gender-Genred Reading." In Mary F. Pharr and Leisa A. Clark, eds., *Of Bread, Blood and* The Hunger Games: *Critical Essays on the Suzanne Collins Trilogy*. Jefferson, NC: McFarland, pp. 118–127.

Lévinas, Emmanuel. 1998. *Otherwise Than Being, Or, Beyond Essence*. Translated by Alphonso Lingis. Pittsburgh, PA: Duquesne University Press.

Lewis, Reina, ed. 2013. *Modest Fashion: Styling Bodies, Mediating Faith*. London; New York: I. B. Tauris.

Lewis, Reina, ed. 2015. *Muslim Fashion: Contemporary Style Cultures*. Durham: Duke University Press.

Lynch, Danielle Anne. 2018. *God in Sound and Silence: Music as Theology*. Eugene, OR: Wipf and Stock Publishers.

Lyon, David. 2001. *Surveillance Society: Monitoring Everyday Life*. Buckingham: Open University Press.

Macaluso, Michael, and Cori McKenzie. 2014. "Exploiting the Gaps in the Fence: Power, Agency, and Rebellion in *The Hunger Games*." In Sean P. Connors, ed., *The Politics of Panem: Challenging Genres*. Rotterdam: Sense Publishers, pp. 103–121.

Madden, Etta M., and Martha L. Finch, eds. 2006. *Eating in Eden: Food and American Utopias*. Lincoln: University of Nebraska Press.

Makins, Marian. 2015. "Refiguring the Roman Empire in The Hunger Games Trilogy." In Brett M. Rogers and Benjamin Eldon Stevens, eds., *Classical Traditions in Science Fiction*. New York: Oxford University Press, pp. 280–306.

Martin, Bruce. 2014. "Political Muttations: Real or Nor Real." In Deirdre Anne Evans Garriott, Whitney Elaine Jones, and Julie Elizabeth Tyler, eds., *Space and Place in* The Hunger Games: *New Readings of the Novels*. Jefferson, NC: McFarland, pp. 220–242.

Mason, Amelia. 2014. "The Hidden Roots Of 'Hunger Games' Hit Song? Murder Ballads, Civil Rights Hymns." (December 10). Wbur.org. URL: https://www.wbur.org/artery/2014/12/10/hunger-games-mockingjay.

McAvan, Emily. 2017. "'May the Odds Be Ever in Your Favour': The Sacrificial Logic of *The Hunger Games*." *The Bible and Critical Theory* Vol. 13, No. 2: 49–62.

McDonald, Brian. 2012. "'The Final Word on Entertainment': Mimetic and Monstrous Art in *The Hunger Games*." In William Irwin, ed., The Hunger Games *and Philosophy: A Critique of Pure Treason*. Hoboken, NJ: John Wiley & Sons, pp. 1–24.

McDonald, Brian. 2014. "The Three Faces of Evil: A Philosophical Reading of *The Hunger Games*." In Sean P. Connors, ed., *The Politics of Panem: Challenging Genres*. Rotterdam: Sense Publishers, pp. 65–84.

McEvoy-Levy, Siobhan. 2018. *Peace and Resistance in Youth Cultures: Reading the Politics of Peacebuilding from* Harry Potter *to* The Hunger Games. London: Palgrave Macmillan.

McGuire, Meredith B. 2008. *Lived Religion: Faith and Practice in Everyday Life*. Oxford University Press.

McNeil, Peter, Vicki Karaminas, and Cathy Cole. 2009. *Fashion in Fiction: Text and Clothing in Literature, Film, and Television*. Oxford, UK; New York: Berg.

Mendlesohn, Farah, and Edward James. 2012. *A Short History of Fantasy*. Oxfordshire: Libri Publishing.

Mills, Sophie. 2015. "Classical Elements and Mythological Archetypes in *The Hunger Games*." *New Voices in Classical Reception Studies* Vol. 10: 56–64.

Montz, Amy L. 2012. "Costuming the Resistance: The Female Spectacle of Rebellion." In Mary F. Pharr and Leisa A. Clark, eds., *Of Bread, Blood and* The Hunger Games: *Critical Essays on the Suzanne Collins Trilogy*. Jefferson, NC: McFarland, pp. 139–147.

Montz, Amy L. 2016. "Rebels in Dresses: Distractions of Competitive Girlhood in Young Adult Dystopian Fiction." In Claudia Nelson, Miranda A. Green-Barteet, and Amy L. Montz, eds., *Female Rebellion in Young Adult Dystopian Fiction*. Farnham, Surrey, UK; Burlington, VT: Ashgate, pp. 121–136.

Morgan, David, ed. 2010. *Religion and Material Culture: The Matter of Belief*. London and New York: Routledge.

Morgan, David, ed. 2012. *The Embodied Eye: Religious Visual Culture and the Social Life of Feeling*. Berkeley: University of California Press.

Morgan, David, ed. 2018. *Images at Work: The Material Culture of Enchantment*. New York: Oxford University Press.

Mortimore-Smith, Shannon R. 2012. "Fueling the Spectacle: Audience as 'Gamemaker.'" In Mary F. Pharr and Leisa A. Clark, eds., *Of Bread, Blood and* The Hunger Games: *Critical Essays on the Suzanne Collins Trilogy*. Jefferson, NC: McFarland, pp. 158–166.

Murnane, Ben. 2018. "Now is a Dystopia: Ayn Rand and the Right-Wing Appropriation of *The Hunger Games*." *The Journal of Popular Culture* Vol. 51, No. 2: 280–301.

Murray, Susan, and Laurie Ouellette, eds. 2009. *Reality TV: Remaking Television Culture*. 2nd Ed. New York: New York University Press.

Nestle, Marion. 2013. *Food Politics: How the Food Industry Influences Nutrition and Health*. Berkeley: University of California Press.

Ouellette, Laurie, and James Hay. 2008. *Better Living Through Reality TV*. Oxford: Blackwell.

Ouellette, Laurie, ed. 2013. *A Companion to Reality Television*. Malden, MA: Wiley-Blackwell.

Parks, Lori L., and Jennifer P. Yamashiro. 2015. "Consumed: Food in *The Hunger Games*." *European Journal of American Culture* Vol. 34, No. 2: 137–150.

Pérez, Elizabeth. 2016. *Religion in the Kitchen: Cooking, Talking, and the Making of Black Atlantic Traditions*. New York: New York University Press.

Piatti-Farnell, Lorna, and Donna Lee Brien, eds. 2018. *The Routledge Companion to Literature and Food*. New York, NY: Routledge.

Plate, S. Brent. 2014. *A History of Religion in 5½ Objects: Bringing the Spiritual to Its Senses*. Boston: Beacon Press.

Poster, Mark. 2007. "Swan's Way: Care of Self in the Hyperreal." *Configurations* Vol. 15, No. 2: 151–175.

Riley, Kathleen C., and Amy L. Paugh. 2018. *Food and Language: Discourses and Foodways Across Cultures*. New York, NY: Routledge.

Ringlestein, Yonah. 2013. "Real or Not Real: *The Hunger Games* as Transmediated Religion." *Journal of Religion and Popular Culture* Vol. 25, No. 3: 372–387.

Rocamora, Agnès, and Anneke Smelik. 2015. "Thinking through Fashion: An Introduction." In Agnès Rocamora and Anneke Smelik, eds., *Thinking Through Fashion: A Guide to Key Theorists*. London: I. B. Tauris, pp. 1–27.

Rocamora, Agnès. 2015. "Pierre Bourdieu: The Field of Fashion." In Agnès Rocamora and Anneke Smelik, eds., *Thinking Through Fashion: A Guide to Key Theorists*. London: I. B. Tauris, pp. 233–250.

Ruthven, Andrea. 2017. "The Contemporary Postfeminist Dystopia: Disruptions and Hopeful Gestures in Suzanne Collins' *The Hunger Games*." *Feminist Review* Vol. 116, No. 1: 47–62.

Sack, Daniel. 2000. *Whitebread Protestants: Food and Religion in American Culture*. New York: St. Martin's Press.

Salzman-Mitchell, Patricia, and Jean Alvares. 2018. "Arrows, Roots, Bread, and Song: Mythical Aspects of *The Hunger Games*." In *Classical Myth and Film in the New Millennium*. New York: Oxford University Press, pp. 279–306.

Silk, Mark. 1984. "Notes on the Judeo-Christian Tradition in America." *American Quarterly* Vol. 36, No. 1: 65–85.

Smyth, Andrew. 2014. "Splicing Genes with Postmodern Teens: *The Hunger Games* and the Hybrid Imagination." In Jeanne Dubino, Ziba Rashidian, and Andrew Smyth, eds., *Representing the Modern Animal in Culture*. New York: Palgrave Macmillan, pp. 177–190.

Soncini, Sara. 2015. "'In Hunger for Bread, Not in Thirst for Revenge': Belly, Bellum and Rebellion in *Coriolanus* and *The Hunger Games* Trilogy." *Altre Modernità* Vol. 13: 100–120.

Sullivan, Anthony. 2014. "'Working for the Few': Fashion, Class and Our Imagined Future in *The Hunger Games*." *Film, Fashion & Consumption* Vol. 3, No. 3: 181–194.

Swanson, Kj. 2016. "Sinners, Saints, and Angels on Fire: The Curiously Religious Soundtrack of *The Hunger Games*' Secular Dystopia." *The Journal of Religion and Popular Culture* Vol. 28, No. 1: 23–42.

Taber, Nancy, Vera Woloshyn, and Laura Lane. 2013. "'She's More like a Guy' and 'He's More Like a Teddy Bear': Girls' Perception of Violence and Gender in *The Hunger Games*." *Journal of Youth Studies* Vol. 16, No. 8 (December): 1022–1037.

Tate, Andrew. 2017. "Keep Watching: Spectacle, Rebellion and Apocalyptic Rites of Passage." In *Apocalyptic Fiction*. London, UK; New York, USA: Bloomsbury Academic, pp. 103–128.

Tigner, Amy L., and Allison Carruth. 2018. *Literature and Food Studies*. Abingdon, Oxon: Routledge.

Torkelson, Anne. 2012. "'Somewhere Between Hair Ribbons and Rainbows': How Even the Shortest Song Can Change the World." In William Irwin, ed., The Hunger Games *and Philosophy: A Critique of Pure Treason*. Hoboken, NJ: John Wiley & Sons, pp. 26–40.

Tseëlon, Efrat. 2015. "Jean Baudrillard: Post-modern Fashion as the End of Meaning." In Agnès Rocamora and Anneke Smelik, eds., *Thinking Through Fashion: A Guide to Key Theorists*. London: I. B. Tauris, pp. 215–232.

Van Dyke, Christina. 2012. "Discipline and the Docile Body: Regulating Hungers in the Capitol." In William Irwin, ed., *The Hunger Games and Philosophy: A Critique of Pure Treason*. Hoboken, NJ: John Wiley & Sons, pp. 250–264.

Vu, Ryan. 2017. "Fantasy After Representation: *D&D, Game of Thrones*, and Postmodern World-Building." *Extrapolation* Vol. 58, No. 2–3: 273–301.

Weber, Lindsey. 2014. "What Is the Origin of *Mockingjay*'s Haunting Song, 'The Hanging Tree'?" (November 24). *Vulture.com*. URL: https://www.vulture.com/2014/11/mockingjay-song-hanging-tree-jennifer-lawrence-explainer.html.

Wezner, Kelley. 2012. "Perhaps I Am Watching You Now: Panem's Panopticons." In Mary F. Pharr and Leisa A. Clark, eds., *Of Bread, Blood and* The Hunger Games: *Critical Essays on the Suzanne Collins Trilogy*. Jefferson, NC: McFarland, pp. 148–157.

Williams, Jeffrey. 2018. "Dying to Save: Child Sacrifice in the *Harry Potter* and *The Hunger Games* Series." *The Journal of Religion and Popular Culture* Vol. 30, No. 2: 75–86.

Wilson, Elizabeth. 1987. *Adorned in Dreams: Fashion and Modernity*. Berkeley: University of California Press.

Wolfe, Gary K. 2011. *Evaporating Genres: Essays on Fantastic Literature*. Middletown, CT: Wesleyan University Press.

Wright, Katheryn. 2012. "Revolutionary Art in the Age of Reality TV." In Mary F. Pharr and Leisa A. Clark, eds., *Of Bread, Blood and* The Hunger Games: *Critical Essays on the Suzanne Collins Trilogy*. Jefferson, NC: McFarland, pp. 98–107.

Zeller, Benjamin E. et al., eds. 2014. *Religion, Food, and Eating in North America*. New York: Columbia University Press.